MODERN SHARKING

MARK SAMPSON

DEDICATION

This book is dedicated to my family, which never seems embarrassed that a member of their clan chases sharks for a living, and to my thousands of charter clients who have faithfully financed my exploits for so many years.

TABLE OF CONTENTS

INTRODUCTION

Many years ago my friends Dick and Rick Arnold, Gary McHugh, and first mate Tim Jones gathered on my boat for a diving trip down in the Florida Keys. We anchored on a reef in about 20 feet of water and spent most of the morning spear fishing and investigating some remains of an old wreck. About noon everyone gathered back on the boat to take a break from the water, grab lunch, and plan the afternoon dive. Tim and Gary were more fishermen than divers so they seized the opportunity to send a bait out out behind the boat for a big barracuda or whatever else might be tooling around back there.

A hogfish that I had speared was filleted, the carcass put on a hook, and the rig sent out with the aid of a kite to keep the bait directly on the surface of the water. Our lunch was interrupted when someone called out "Shark on the kite!" And we all looked to see a foot and a half of dorsal fin cutting past the bait.

The shape and size of the fin told me it was a great hammerhead, not a monster, but at nine feet and about 300 pounds it was pretty hefty! Before the shark slipped out of sight its non-aggressive body language and the fact that it didn't eat the bait gave me an idea. Dick had brought along an underwater video camera, and I told the gang that if the fish showed again I'd hop in the water and try to get it on film. I remember some of my crew not being so keen of my plan and at least one gave me the old "not even you're that crazy" speech. Their skepticism only strengthened my commitment.

I didn't have much time to ponder what I was contemplating because, within a minute or two of making the pledge, the shark popped back up behind the boat. As quickly as I could I slipped on my mask and fins, grabbed the video camera, a pole-spear (as a poking tool in case the shark got too "friendly") and slipped into the water.

At first I couldn't see the shark, so I hovered at the surface about 20 feet from our hogfish bait, waiting and watching. And then, there it was! The hammerhead was directly below me and cruising just off the bottom. I clicked on the camera, got a few seconds of film, and then it was gone. I waited a couple minutes for the shark to reappear but even when I swam to the bottom I couldn't see it, so I figured that rather than push my luck I'd better head back to the boat. Resurfacing, I was just about to strike off in the direction of the boat when I heard someone aboard say, "there he is" and I knew they weren't talking about me. With my head above the water I turned around and saw the shark's fin cutting a straight wake, and behind it the tail swayed back and forth leaving a meandering surface trail of its own. I clicked the camera and pointed it in the direction of the shark while I strained to see it underwater. At first, nothing. I knew it was there but I just couldn't see it.

To look down and see the shark swimming across the bottom was pretty cool, but I'll admit that when I knew that it was now up on the surface, at my level, my mind was suddenly prompted to recall some of the more grisly facts about great hammerheads that I didn't contemplate before leaving the boat. It's a species with a not-so-good reputation! But I also remembered that I got in the water because, at least by my experience, the shark looked okay.

With the camera running I struggled to catch a glimpse of the shark that I knew was close, but where? And suddenly, there it was, 40 feet out and swimming directly towards me—or should I say, at me. At least that's the way it felt as I watched the shark's approach, its big head swaying from side-to-side in rhythm with each sweep of its three foot long tail, mouth slightly agape, a couple remoras clinging to its belly. Good or bad, it was the most impressive sight I had ever seen while in the water.

I could tell the hammerhead really was coming to me, it wasn't just swimming along and by coincidence I was in its path, and as he approached I knew the big fellow was using his full array of sensory receptors to figure me out. Sight, sound, smell, vibrations, electro-signature—heck he probably knew what I tasted like before I even saw him. And he kept coming; 30 feet, 25, 20, 15, and as I raised the pole spear to prod him away I remember telling myself, "Okay Sampson, you think you know so much about sharks, you asked for this and now here you are–I hope you're right!"

I still had the camera rolling and was just starting to reach out with the spear when at about eight feet it turned sharply to my right and headed over to the bait that was still dangling below the kite. I followed the shark with the camera and was able to get a shot of it rolling slightly on its side as it grabbed the bait, swam about 10 feet below the surface, spit out the bait, and then vanished.

That little experience occurred back in 1990, and I hadn't really thought much about it until recently when I stumbled upon the video while working on this book. I thought it might be fun to include the story somewhere in the chapters but couldn't quite figure out where to place it. After all, no one is going gain much insight on sharks or shark fishing from the incident, other than maybe that a hammerhead would rather eat a hogfish carcass than a 183 pound charter boat captain, and frankly I'm still trying to decide if I should be happy about that or take that as an insult.

So I finished the entire book except for this Introduction, which I let go 'till last so I'd know what the heck the book was all about before I tried to introduce it. But while proofreading my creation I came to the realization that the content is likely to ruffle the feathers of a couple very different groups of readers, and I know that sooner or later my written words will have me facing the jaws of any such skeptics.

Thirty-five years ago folks who had never seen saltwater before were following Hollywood's suggestions that the only good shark was a dead shark. These days, led by overly-sympathetic television documentaries and even some animal rights groups, this same group has done a 180 and now wouldn't hurt a shark if it was chewing their legs off. I don't suppose they'll be happy to see this book! I suppose that even some fishermen will view this book on the rack and wince at the thought of someone giving instructions on how to catch sharks. And in a time when some shark populations around the world have been decimated by so many years of unrestricted fishing, I can see how those who have a genuine concern for our ocean's ecosystem would have such reservations.

But this book is not about shark fishing using all the techniques, tactics, and ethics that helped contribute to the decline of so many of these marvelous predators. Unlike the old days, when sport fishermen chased sharks with the ambition of dragging home the biggest, meanest looking sharks they could get their hooks into solely for a few "hero" pictures at the dock and a couple teeth to wear around their necks, *Modern Sharking* is about "sustainable" shark fishing where anglers pursue sharks armed not only with rods, reels, and a bucket of chum, but also a higher level of knowledge and respect for the many species of sharks that reside off our coastlines. *Modern Sharking* is about anglers always putting the welfare of sharks first, and only then enjoying whatever sport and responsible harvest can be derived from these magnificent animals without adversely impacting their populations.

Modern Sharking starts by introducing the reader to sharks from a biological standpoint. No, this is not a biology book, but I'm a firm believer that to be a better fisherman you've got to know your quarry inside and out, so in the first chapter we take a quick look at life history, reproduction, physical characteristics, and the sharks incredible sensory system. Chapter two is a bit more of a history lesson about the relationship between man and shark, and as you might have guessed, the "good old days" were a lot better for the fishermen than they were for the sharks!

Chapter three includes a summary description of 20 species of sharks anglers might encounter off the East Coast and in the Gulf of Mexico, discussing biology, locations, seasons, and fishing techniques. After that, the book slips more into "how-to" mode where in each chapter I give a pretty thorough description on what you've got to do to catch a shark these days. Perhaps even more important, the stern of the book deals a lot with what to do with a shark once you get him to the boat. Here we look at reasons to boat or release sharks and exactly how to do both, as well as cleaning, cooking, and how to mount a set of jaws. Throughout the book I've weaved in a number of my true-life experiences, if for no other reason than to help the reader learn from my own bumbling mistakes and better understand how much this sport has progressed over the years.

The best way I can summarize what *Modern Sharking* is all about is to relay just one more short story: In the winter of 2007 I was fishing in the Florida Keys with my wife Charlotte. She had a goal to set a new IGFA world record on fly tackle. So for almost a month we pushed our boat around the shallow flats hoping to find a cooperative shark of the right proportions. One afternoon everything "clicked" and she had her prize to the boat. Since IGFA rules allow anglers to measure, weigh, and document their own fish providing they do so on a certified scale, fishermen are often able to release their catch and still qualify for the record. Having set records before, Charlotte and I had the needed equipment ready so that any shark could be processed and back in the water in a timely manor without any ill-effects from the encounter.

Everything had gone as rehearsed until I was about to release the shark and realized that I didn't get a photo of it with the tackle. As I plucked the shark back out of the water for one more camera shot Charlotte made a statement that not only reminded me why I married the girl, but also typified an attitude that I wish all fishermen would have the guts and the ethics to embrace. Charlotte said to me, "You've got to hurry up and get it back in the water—no record is worth killing that shark for!"

We probably all know folks who would kill their own mother for a world record; fortunately, these days there are a lot more anglers who have either cast off or have never been infected by the "old ways" that allow ego to dictate which fish will live and which will die. Sharks can and should be enjoyed by recreational anglers, but with all the damage man has inflicted on shark populations over the years, it's now time for those of us who participate in this fishery to increase our respect, understanding, and concern for these incredible predators. I hope you'll find that's what *Modern Sharking* is all about.

In the same way that I plunged into the water with the hammerhead that day, I dove into the writing of this book confident that the outcome would turn out well, because after more than three decades of standing watch over chum lines, running shark tournaments, working with biologists, chasing IGFA records, and guiding thousands of clients to their own unique shark encounters, I feel quite certain that I know what I'm talking about. As it was with the hammerhead, I anticipate the approach of critics who, even though they could rip this book (and me) to shreds, if they read it through and understand my message, will take the right turn and go for the hogfish instead.

CHAPTER 1

Shark Basics

Sharks and rays are in a group known as "elasmobranchs" which are defined as fish with an internal skeleton comprised of carti- lage instead of bone, and that have five to seven gill openings. There are more than 350 species of sharks and over 400 species of rays. Although their outward appearance is quite different sharks and rays have a lot in common, it's just that somewhere in their journey down the evolutionary highway the rays' bodies flattened out, their pectoral fins widened and took over the task of propulsion, which give their tail a chance to shrivel down to a whip-like appendage that trails behind the fish as it swims. Sharks kept their tails, round bodies, and obvi- ously – their rather infamous teeth! Somewhere between the sharks and rays are the sawfishes and guitarfishes. With their ray-like front half and shark-like back half, these species don't appear to have completed the conversion quite yet.

Reproduction

Most folks have probably heard about how sharks have re- mained unchanged for millions of years. Sharks have done so well, for so long, in part because of their unique reproductive systems. Most fish reproduce by laying large numbers of eggs, which are then fertilized externally. Since the developing young can only be nour- ished by the small amount of yolk contained within the egg, they hatch in a relatively short amount of time and are typically very small in relation to the size of their parents. High mortality rates occur during development of both eggs and young fish, which are very vulnerable to predation by other marine creatures and adverse environmental factors. Consider the salmon, tuna, billfish, menhaden – lots of little ones are produced, but only a few ever make it to adulthood.

Sharks on the other hand have survived for so many millions of years because rather than going for big numbers, sharks have big babies or "pups" instead. After internal fertilization, shark embryos typically develop inside the mother. This offers the pups protection during their development and allows them to be born at a relatively large size, usually as exact miniature replicas of their parents. The larger size at birth gives the pups a better chance of survival; there's an awful lot of little critters in the ocean that can easily snap up a tiny half-inch tuna or blue marlin, but a newborn 36" dusky shark only has to worry about being eaten by the larger predators.

Sharks reproduce in one of three ways; oviparity, viviparity, and ovoviviparity. Oviparous sharks such as nurse sharks and the giant whale sharks lay eggs which are enclosed in thick, almost leathery cases, that are deposited on the bottom. The eggs are similar to the skate egg cases found floating on the ocean and local waterways. They have long tendrils that attach to bottom plants, rocks, or debris. The eggs contain enough yolk to nourish the young until they become fully developed and eventually hatch. The size of the egg, however, limits the size of the yolk sack and, therefore, the amount of nutrients available to a pup during development. This results in oviparous pups being proportionately smaller than those produced via other forms shark reproduction.

Unlike most sharks, nurse sharks lay eggs which hatch externally.

Like all viviparous sharks, this smooth hammerhead was nourished via an umbilical cord until it was eventually born alive.

Unlike sharks, most fish, like this dolphin, produce
thousands of offspring each year.

Viviparous sharks develop inside the mother until they are eventually born alive and fully capable of fending for themselves. The pups begin their development by being nourished via a small yolk sack on a long yolk cord. When the yolk is used up the empty sack attaches to the mother's uterus and transforms into an umbilical cord, which then provides nourishment to the pup until it's born alive. Some sharks that reproduce using viviparity include the duskies, blues, sandbars, smooth dogfish, and hammerheads.

While still inside its mother, the "ovoviviparous" spiny dogfish first hatches from a thin egg case and is then nourished by a yolk sack before being born fully developed.

Even at less than a year old, young sharks like this spinner pup have fewer
predators to worry about than most fish their same age.

The third method of shark reproduction is known as ovoviviparity. The eggs of ovoviviparous sharks, which do not have the
tough leathery cases of the oviparous sharks, hatch in the uterus
while the young are still only partially developed. As they continue to
grow, the pups are then nourished by their own yolk sack. Once this
yolk sack is used up they're fully developed and born alive. Some
ovoviviparous sharks like sand tigers and threshers use up their yolk
sacks quickly and then nourish themselves by eating both unfertil-
ized eggs and their smaller siblings. This form of cannibalization is
known as oviphagy. Mako and great white sharks also reproduce by
ovoviviparity.

Shark Senses

The two obvious nostrils under the nose of a shark are its long-range prey detectors. Just as winds carry smells through the air, ocean currents can transmit scent miles through the water and provide faraway sharks with the first indication that a potential meal lies ahead. Like a bloodhound working its way along a fresh scent trail, once acquiring a whiff of something good a shark can track the aroma to the source and maybe its next meal.

As they get closer to their prey, a shark will eventually get within "ear-shot" of whatever it's tracking. Sound is easily transmitted underwater and sharks are especially adept at picking up on the low frequency sounds often produced by injured or struggling fish. Sharks don't have external ears like most animals, but that surely doesn't mean they can't hear what's going on in their watery home. Almost directly above the eyes and at the center of their head are two pin-hole size openings that are the start of the ear canals.

Scent and sound will bring these predators awfully close to their prey, but there would be a lot skinny sharks out there if those were the only two senses they could rely on to put food in their mouth. Most fish have what is known as a "lateral line" running from gill to tail down the middle of each side. On sharks this line is comprised of tiny, fluid-filled canals with hair-like receptors that pick up vibrations in the water. As they get closer to their prey, these receptors help sharks to discern more information about where their target is located, as well as additional details about the nature of their quarry and whether it's casually swimming, fleeing, injured, or struggling.

You certainly don't have to look at too many different species to realize there are a lot of variations going on in the eyes of sharks. And the eyes themselves can give clues about the nature of the sharks that peer through them. The mako's big black eyes would suggest a fish that lives and hunts in clean, clear, offshore waters where good eyesight is an important asset. But to sharks such as the sand tiger that lives much closer to shore in an environment where the water may often be too murky to see even a few feet, tiny eyes are not much of a liability. Specialized cells within shark's eyes are known to actually reflect light back to the retina and greatly enhance

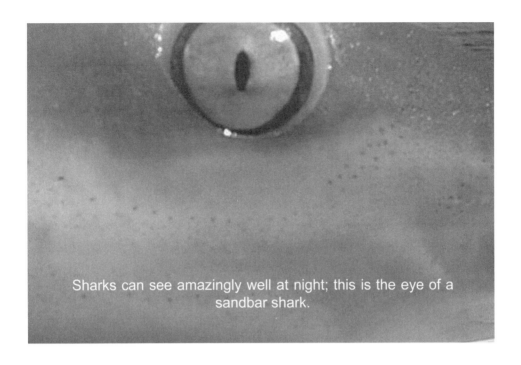

Sharks can see amazingly well at night; this is the eye of a sandbar shark.

Armed with an array of senses to locate prey, sharks like this blacknose seldom go hungry.

their vision in the dark.

All those wonderful senses come together to bring a shark within striking range of its prey, but it still has to know precisely where and when to close its jaws, and for that they have an incredible array of sensory receptors known as "ampullae of Lorenzini," which are hundreds of tiny pores located on and below the head and snout of every shark. The ampullae are filled with an electro-conductive jelly-like substance that can actually pick up the minute electrical fields generated by living creatures in the water. The ampullae appear as small pinholes, that are spread about the head and jaw area and often follow symmetrical patterns.

Even though sharks often lose sight of prey as it passes under their nose, with their electro sensory abilities they're able to verify not only the exact location of a chunk of meat as it passes beneath them, but also a fish in total darkness, or a crab buried under the sand.

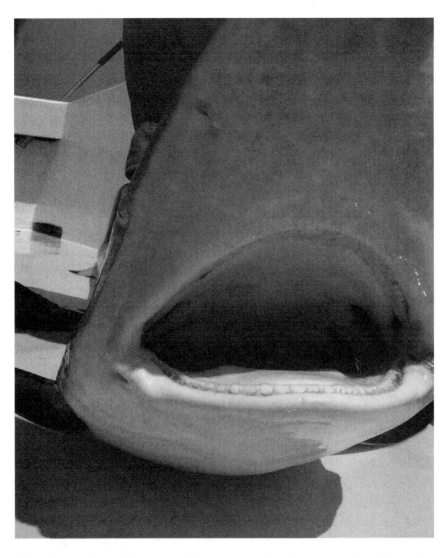

The "ampullae of Lorenzini" located under its nose tells this spinner shark just where to bite.

Males and Females

There are not too many fish that the average angler can look at and tell beyond a doubt if it's a male or female, but with sharks it's easy – male sharks have "claspers," and females do not. Located on either side of the anal opening, the pelvic fins are the last "pair" of fins before the tail. In male sharks the trailing edge of these fins are modified into two sex organs that are easily observed when viewing a shark from below. The claspers act as channels for the sperm and during breeding they turn forward and one is inserted into the female.

The claspers on young sharks are less obvious because they are no longer than the pelvic fins. As a shark ages and becomes sexually mature the claspers grow out beyond pelvic fins and become very noticeable appendages.

The claspers on this mature mako are easy to identify as they project beyond the pelvic fins.

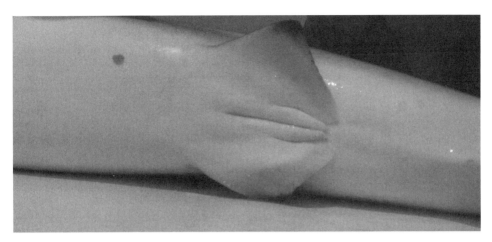

The claspers of an immature spinner shark.

Teeth – Jaws

Just like other physical characteristics, a comparison of the teeth of different species not only exposes incredible diversity in the size and design of the tooth, it also reveals clues to the feeding habits of various sharks. The long, thin, smooth-sided teeth of the sand tiger indicate a shark designed to quickly lash out and snag relatively small prey that can be swallowed in one piece. Makos also have long snagging-type teeth, but they're a bit broader and have a sharp cutting edge on either side. Such dentures are stronger than the sand tiger's and allow the mako to quickly snag its prey and then, with just a couple shakes of its head, slice it down to bite-size pieces. Of course, it would be hard to find a better tool for tearing very large prey down to size than the wide serrated teeth and massive jaws of the great white.

Tiger sharks have a very broad, strong tooth, set in a huge jaw. The design allow these sharks to crunch their way through the hard sea turtle shells that would easily shatter most other sharks teeth. Despite their sometimes enormous size, thresher sharks have tiny teeth in a small jaw designed to grab and swallow small schooling fish after they have been whacked and stunned with the sharks unique tail.

Then there's the common multi-purpose design found in the bull, dusky, sandbar and so many other sharks that feature broad serrated slicing teeth in the top jaw with thin snagging and holding teeth in the bottom. And I dare not leave out the smooth dogfish. Although it has more teeth than most sharks, they're designed for crushing small crustaceans so there's not a sharp one in its mouth.

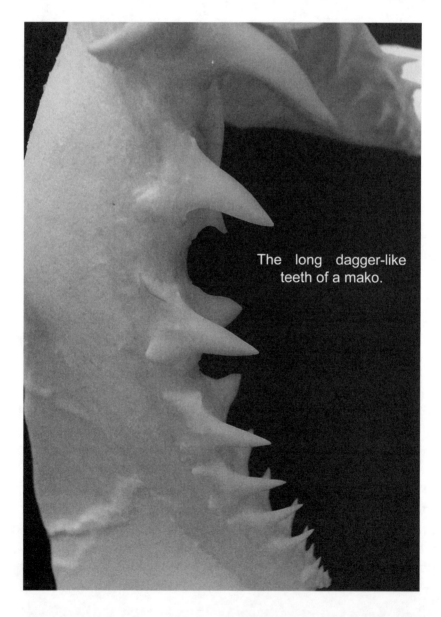

The long dagger-like teeth of a mako.

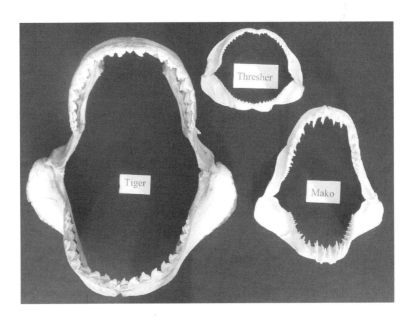

The variations of size and design of tooth and jaw speaks to
the different feeding habits of each species.

CHAPTER 2

Sharks and Man

What is it about sharks that intrigues so many people? After all – they're just fish. Sure they get really big, but so do elephants. They offer fishermen some incredible angling opportunities, but so do bluegill and blue marlin. They've been known to kill and eat people, but so have lions and grizzly bears.

Why have I received calls and letters from across the country and emails from around the world from people with questions and comments about sharks? Why do people, who have no interest in fishing, travel hundreds of miles and pay me to take them offshore to see sharks? And how is it that a fictional Hollywood movie from the 70's continues to effect peoples' perception of the ocean and the life within after more than 30 years? Why are so many people of all ages, many of whom have never even seen the ocean let alone set foot in it, absolutely flip-flop nutzo over sharks?

The fact is: I haven't got a clue! But I know it's something that was going on long before the book *JAWS* (yeah, there was a book first) and even before Jacques Cousteau's stories and images of sharks ever made from the deck of his *Calypso* to the rabbit-ears on our living room television sets. I also know that "it" grabbed me when I was in fourth grade and able to darn-near memorize every book about sharks in our elementary school library. It had me long before I had set foot on the first boat that would take me offshore to see a real shark, and I guess it still has me – and apparently a whole lot of other people too.

This love-hate-fear thing man has had for these animals hasn't been too good for the sharks. Particularly early on when man's infatuation with sharks led to an awful lot of them swinging from a pole at the end of a dock. Some guy in Iowa wants a set of jaws—dead shark. Someone in Europe wants a pair of shark-skin boots—dead shark. Someone in New Jersey wants a shark steak for dinner—dead shark.

The folks in Japan decide they like shark fin soup—dead species!

But it would seem that things are ever so slowly getting better. It wasn't too many years ago that there were no catch restrictions on sharks anywhere on the planet. While this still the case in too many countries, there now are varying levels of shark management in more than just the industrialized nations. And children these days are growing up with the opportunity to see documentaries on sharks that actually have an education and conservation theme, rather than simply sensationalized accounts of shark attacks. I've also noticed that many of the kids I take out on my boat tend to be more accepting of catch-and-release than their parents; somewhere they're getting the message that having a great day on the water has nothing to do

Small boat anglers continue to play a big role in the recreational shark fishery.

with whether or not they bring something home in the cooler. Then again, maybe it's just because the youngsters don't have to pay their household grocery bill!

Recreational Shark Fishing

Sport fishing for sharks has gone through a series of transitions since I got started with it back in the early 70's. Even as a kid working at a busy marina who knew a lot of captains and private boat owners who fished offshore, I was hard pressed to find anyone who could tell me anything more about how to catch a shark than, "use steel leader." At least that simple response was better than the usual,

Nowhere is man's fascination with sharks more evident than at fishing tournaments.

"what the heck do you want to catch a shark for?"

Since we couldn't find anyone to show us how, a few friends and I used to just go out and wing it. We experimented with bait, chum, tackle, locations, and every other facet of the sport. While we didn't know it at the time, we certainly weren't alone in our experimentation or our growing passion for the sport of shark fishing. The same thing was going on all along the coast, but in a time before the sportsmens' channels and the Internet, word just didn't get around so fast.

The 70's was a time when increasingly reliable outboards and sturdy center console boats were just beginning to allow fishermen to confidently fish farther offshore than ever before, and small boat anglers everywhere were pushing their limits and chasing bigger fish. But along much of the coast, including my home state of Maryland, to reach the popular marlin, tuna, dolphin, and wahoo grounds required a longer ride out than many small boaters (like myself) equipped with little more than a single engine, CB radio, and (of course) no loran, were ready to make. Nonetheless, members of the "mosquito-fleet" wanted to catch big fish, and if we couldn't get way offshore to catch the glory fish we were content to stay closer to shore and fish for sharks.

Back then we used to get a lot of flack from the owners of larger boats, who called us crazy to go offshore in such small boats. I remember being a little hesitant to tell some of them that we were fishing for sharks – they didn't approve of that either. Finally I realized that since they already thought we were crazy for going out in small boats, we might as well seal the deal by letting them know we're going shark fishing, too.

As time went on, small boat anglers who started out sharking as an alternative to fishing for something else began to realize how much fun it really was, and before long a lot of them forgot all about that "something else" and were perfectly content to stay focused on sharks and improve their techniques. And they caught a lot of sharks. They caught some very large sharks. The word spread, more fishermen got into sharking, and the press picked up on the whole "big fish from small boat" theme. When shark tournaments started to pop up along the coast, the public really started to take notice and more

It doesn't always take a large shark to impress young people.

folks wanted in on the fun. But a lot of them didn't have boats, so they started to hire boats to go sharking, which meant that, whether they liked it or not, a lot of big-boat charter captains who wanted no part of shark fishing before were now getting dragged into the sport – sometimes kicking and screaming all the way, but with people at the dock waving money at them they didn't really have much choice!

Coincidently, while all this was going on, and as if designed to fan the flames and keep everyone riled-up about sharks, sequels from the movie *JAWS* kept popping up every few years. By the mid to late 80's recreational shark fishing was in its heyday as both private and charter boats of all sizes were now fully engaged in the fishery. At the time we seemed to have an abundance of sharks and virtually no regulations. A lot of boat policies back then were "catch what you can, bring home what you want, and figure out what to do with it later." Too often, after posing for hero shots back at the dock, some crews would finally "release" their catch (minus its jaws) and allow it drift back to the ocean on the outgoing tide.

The problem, at least for a while, was that there was suddenly a whole lot of shark-catching but not much shark-respecting going on. Not all, but certainly way too many recreational shark fishermen, stayed so focused on what they could catch in that they didn't pay much mind to what they should catch, and shark populations took a hit from it all.

By the 1990's the popularity of recreational shark fishing finally began to simmer down to a more reasonable level. Sharks were still a desirable quarry for a lot of anglers but they were no longer such a novelty back at the dock. Sport fishermen were finally beginning to recognize sharks as a valuable but limited resource that, just like other game fish, required at least some level of conservation. During this period the federal government also got involved when the NMFS initiated the first federal shark management plan, placing catch limits for sharks on both recreational and commercial fishermen.

It took a while, but as ethics and attitudes toward sharks progressed and more restrictive government regulations took effect, recreational shark fishing evolved into the primarily catch-and-release fishery that it is today. Sure, there are still some bad actors out there who abuse the resource without regard or regret. But overall,

recreational shark fishermen have evolved into a pretty good lot who have as much concern for the well-being of the sharks they pursue as they do for the sport itself.

Commercial Shark Fishing

Around the globe many populations of sharks are in trouble. For too many years, too many countries have allowed unrestricted harvest of sharks off their coastline either because they have no regulations or they don't enforce the regulations that they have. Since the 90's U.S. commercial shark fishermen have operated under regulations that were more restrictive than a lot of countries, but still not restrictive enough to prevent many of the species that they target to become overfished. Very recently, tighter regulations have gone into effect that will likely drive a lot of folks out of the shark business, and severely restrict the operations and landings of those who stay involved with it. And that's a good thing, because the simple biology of sharks does not allow their populations to withstand being harvested at commercials levels. Just like the commercial market-hunting for waterfowl, deer, and buffalo that occurred in this country so many years ago, commercial shark fishing is a practice that's proven to be unsustainable by the natural limits of the resource. And just like market-hunting, commercial shark fishing must also come to an end.

Unfortunately, due to the highly migratory nature of many shark species, the sharks we protect in our home waters are still in great peril of being taken by foreign fishermen outside the 200-mile buffer zone around our country's coastline (known as the Exclusive Economic Zone, or EEZ).

Eventually recreational shark anglers began to realize that only some species are fit to bring back to the dock.

CHAPTER 3

The Species

Atlantic Sharpnose *(Rhizoprionodon terraenovae)*

I don't expect we'll ever see the day when the glossy cover of some big-time fishing magazine is graced by a photo of an angler holding an Atlantic sharpnose shark. The little guys might be popular, but they just aren't that prestigious. Atlantic sharpnose are a small species of shark that is quite common year-round in the nearshore and sometimes inshore waters from the Carolinas to Florida

The Atlantic sharpnose is a small species that provides light tackle fun for nearshore anglers.

and all along the Gulf Coast. As the waters warm in mid to late summer, these sharks extend their range north to cover most of the East Coast.

Atlantic sharpnose have a habit of congregating in specific areas and forming large groups of similar size and sex, so when anglers catch one of these little sharks, they had better be ready to deal with a whole bunch of its brothers or sisters before the day is out! Most of the Atlantic sharpnose taken by recreational fishermen have a total length of less than four feet and weigh under15 pounds. Yea, they're small by shark standards, but these little sharks can be just the ticket for recreational anglers armed with light tackle who want some simple fun close to shore.

Because of their small size Atlantic sharpnose are sometimes confused by fishermen as smooth dogfish. But that's not a good mistake to make because unlike the dogfish, sharpnose have quite a set

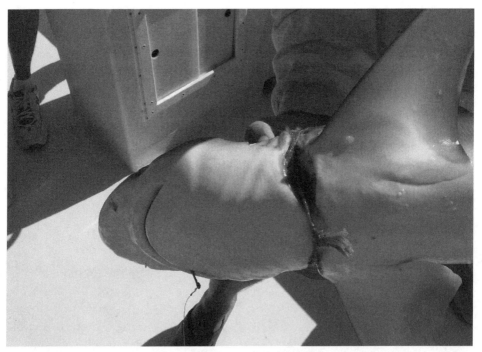

This shark had lived with a section of commercial netting gear around its neck, until we caught it and cut the netting away

of teeth, and a bite by one of these sharks will put an end to a fishing trip real quick! Sharpnose can be recognized by the distinctive white splotchy dots across their bronze back and sides, and by an obvious white fringe along the trailing edge of the pectoral fins.

Blue Shark *(Prionace glauca)*

Whether someone is actually catching them or just watching a handful of blue sharks swim around the boat and nip at the chum bucket, these sharks are just plain fun to have in the chum line because they'll always keep a crew entertained. The blue shark's range covers the entire Atlantic and Gulf of Mexico, but they're primarily taken by recreational anglers in the Mid-Atlantic and Northeast region.

Blue sharks are a pelagic species that seldom stray far from

Blue sharks are known for their long, thin, almost "snake-like" bodies.

the clear, deep waters beyond the continental shelf. However, just like makos, a good source of food can sometimes be enough to prompt these sharks to leave their deep-water haunts and move up on the shelf. In the Mid-Atlantic region this occurs for a relatively short period from late May until about mid-June, when blue sharks join makos along the 20-fathom line. But while makos will occasionally move into even shallower water, the blues almost never will.

Blue sharks have a very dark blue back that transitions to a lighter blue coming on the sides and eventually changes to a snow-white belly. Two characteristics that stand out and help anglers identify these sharks in the water include their very long pectoral fins and a relatively thin body, a combination that often has observers commenting that they resemble little airplanes going through the water. Inexperienced shark fishermen will sometimes look at the slightly pointed nose of a blue shark and wonder if maybe they've caught a mako. Such uncertainty can be easily cleared up by looking at the teeth. A blue shark has short triangular teeth that hook slightly to the

When brought close to the boat blue sharks will often roll up in the leader.

side and are not visible when the mouth is closed; a mako's teeth are long, thin, and easily seen even with the mouth closed.

Blue sharks provide anglers with a decent fight, the strength and duration of which is pretty much dictated by the size of the shark. To get much sport out of blues under 150 pounds, angler will want to hook them up on tackle of 30 pounds or less. Larger blue sharks up to 300 pounds do well on 50-pound-class tackle, much larger than that and anglers might want to consider using 80-pound tackle so as not to drag the fight out too long.

Blue sharks have a frustrating habit of rolling up in the leader while anglers are trying to hold them alongside the boat for tagging, photos, or de-hooking. There's little a fisherman can do to prevent this other than try to rotate the leader in the same direction the fish is rolling so it doesn't get wrapped any more than can be avoided. After it stops spinning, anglers should always make the effort to unwrap a blue shark before release.

One of the most unique things about blue sharks is their habit of swimming up close to boats. When in good blue shark territory it's not at all uncommon to have half a dozen or more blues swimming around the boat and periodically snapping at the chum bucket. At such times anglers have the opportunity to bait and hook individual sharks a few feet from the boat. When they get tired of catching them, anglers can have fun, and get some good action photos, by tying a large bait or fish carcass to a length of cord, hanging it off the side of the boat, and then just watching as the sharks come in to feed on it.

Blacktip *(Carcharhinus limbatus)* & Spinner *(Carcharhinus brevipinna)*

For no other reasons than to save a little ink and not be redundant I'm lumping blacktips and spinners together. I can do this because they are very similar in appearance, range, and habits, but anglers must keep in mind that these are indeed two separate species, and it would serve any shark fisherman well to know how to tell one from the other. But first the similarities.

While they are sometimes encountered far offshore, most anglers hook blacktip and spinner sharks in the shallower nearshore waters close to the coast, sometimes right from the surf or at the mouth of inlets. I'll often refer to these species as "warm water" sharks because off the Mid-Atlantic we don't start seeing them until mid-summer when our local water temperatures push up into the mid-70's, and then they depart once things start to cool in the early fall. These species are somewhat uncommon catches in the Northeast (particularly the spinners), but from the Carolinas south and all along the Gulf Coast, they're quite common throughout most of the year.

Blacktips and spinners dine primarily on small schooling fish. They have a feeding technique that has them spinning and snapping as they charge through schools of their prey. When feeding on schools that occur close to the surface it's not uncommon to see these sharks launch out of the water (still spinning) at the end of an attack. Once hooked, they'll often use the same spinning motion both below the surface and in the air when they jump. On the appropriate tackle both blacktips and spinners are strong, fast, exciting fighters that will never disappoint the angler.

Both blacktips and spinners are grayish bronze in color with a white belly. Adults will usually display a conspicuous Z-shaped swath of white and gray on each side. Both species have a snout that from the top appears less rounded than that of the dusky, sandbar, and bull shark.

While there are a lot of similarities there are also a few subtle differences that will help anglers distinguish these two species. Spinners will grow a bit larger and reach a total length of about nine feet, while blacktips will only make it to six or seven. A profile view of the two sharks will show that a spinner's head from the tip of the nose to the back of its mouth is much sleeker than that of the blacktip; it almost looks as thought the shark's head was put in a press and squashed down to make it more streamlined. A blacktip may also appear to be a bit huskier in the shoulder area just in front of the first dorsal fin.

The first dorsal fin on a spinner is also a little farther back on the body than on a blacktip. But the most obvious distinguishing characteristic involves the black tips on the fins. Both species have black tips on their fins including the bottom lobe of the tail, but the blacktip lacks this marking on the anal fin, which is the last fin on the

Blacktips are often found in water only a few feet deep.

Spinner sharks are sleeker and their black markings more prominent than the blacktip.

underside of the shark before its tail. So the spinner has a black tip on its anal fin, and blacktip does not. Furthermore, the black markings on all the other fins on the spinner are much more noticeable than those of the blacktip – and when blacktips reach maturity, their black tips tend to fade altogether. I know all that sounds kind of backwards, that you'd think from its name that the blacktip would have the more prominent markings, but that's simply not the case.

Blacktips and particularly spinners will sometimes congregate in large groups when baitfish are abundant, and it's not uncommon to have a whole gang of them chummed up. While they usually won't come right up to the boat, they will hold 20 or more yards back and eagerly snap up every bait sent back to them. Events like that make for ideal opportunities to hook them up on plugs, surface poppers, or fly tackle.

The shallow flats and backcountry of the Florida Keys provide year-round opportunities to tangle with medium to large blacktip

Blacktips can't dive in three feet of water – but they sure can run!

sharks. In the clear water anglers can spot their quarry first, and then engage the sharks with whatever tackle is most appropriate for the size blacktip (or other species) that has been attracted by the chum. Light tackle anglers will find that as long as they can follow the shark with the boat, the shallow water can prove to be quite an asset in the fight, as the fish cannot use the depths as a refuge.

Spiny Dogfish *(Squalus acanthias)*

Preferring water below 55-degrees, spiny dogfish can be found in parts of the Northeast almost all year, but in the Mid-Atlantic region they're only around from about November through May. They frequent both offshore and nearshore waters or wherever there are concentrations of bait or bottom fish. Anglers will find that these sharks will happily snap up just about any cut bait they drop over, and will also respond to jigs or deep-diving artificial lures. When the

Light tackle is the only tackle to use for spiny dogfish.

sharks are abundant, it's not uncommon to have a half dozen or more follow a hooked fish right up to the boat.

Recreational anglers will find that these "horndogs" are not much of a fight unless they're hooked on ultra-light tackle. But in the off season when anglers just want to get out and catch something they'll at least put a bend in the rod and are actually pretty good to eat. When filleted and skinned a spiny dogfish will provide a long, narrow fillet of white meat that can then be crosscut into perfect size portions. It can be cooked in just about any fashion, but folks should know that in Europe this shark is often battered and fried to make the popular fish-and-chips. If you like to fry fish, this is the one to use!

Spiny dogfish are brownish gray with a few small white spots on their back and sides. They have very small teeth, but unlike the smooth dogfish the teeth are quite sharp and will easily cut an ill-placed finger or hand. Something else anglers need to be careful with are the spines in front of each of the two dorsal fins. These spines are very sharp and can easily impale someone (even right through a rubber boot) when the fish is freshly caught and still thrashing and kicking about the deck.

Smooth Dogfish *(Mustelus canis)*

The smooth dogfish or "sand shark" (as it's often known) is similar to its cousin the spiny dogfish in that it's a small shark that's caught accidentally by bottom fishermen more often than by anyone on purpose. But that's about where the similarities end. Smooth dog-fish are a little nearshore shark species that grows to about five feet and has a range that covers pretty much the entire East Coast and Gulf of Mexico. Unlike the spiny, smooth dogfish cannot tolerate the colder water temperatures so they move north in the spring and sum-mer months and then retreat to their southern haunts in the fall.

These sharks are about as "kid friendly" as you can get. They don't have dorsal spines to stick you, their skin isn't so rough that it will scratch you, and their teeth are so small and blunt that they can't even bite you. They're primarily bottom dwellers that feed mostly on small crustaceans, but they'll take just about any bait they can get in their mouth. Spiny dogfish are frequently taken in the nearshore

Smooth dogfish or "sand sharks" will grow to five feet, but they're usually caught when they're less than 18 inches.

----

waters and are common catches in the surf and back bays as well.

Dusky *(Carcharhinus obscurus)*

Duskies are about as generic a shark as you can get. Gray/ brown back, white belly, rounded nose, average size eyes, average size triangular teeth, average dorsal, no spots or other markings – that's a dusky. They're sleek, beautiful, strong fighting sharks that might be found in the surf or out along the edge of the continental shelf, they're always fun to catch, and sometimes a handful to work with. But there's just nothing out of the ordinary about this species, like I said – generic! I suppose it's because duskies are so basic that a lot of anglers for a lot of years have come to use the name "dusky" to describe any shark they can't easily identify.

The dusky's range covers most of the East Coast and the Gulf of Mexico. They're very opportunistic feeders and will eat just about anything they get inside their rather large jaws, including fish, rays, crustaceans, squid, and other sharks. Anglers can expect to hook

After the battle it's a quick photo, a tag, and then get that shark out of my little boat!

----

duskies on any kind of bait and at any depth.

Duskies get big – really big, like 12 feet and over 700 pounds! But recreational angers seldom have the opportunity to encounter duskies of those proportions because thanks to overfishing, their numbers have dwindled critically in the past few decades and earned them a place on the NMFS Prohibited Species List, reserving them for catch-and-release only. These days most recreationally caught dusky sharks are hooked in the nearshore waters and are juveniles under 100 pounds.

Sandbar *(Carcharhinus plumbeus)*

With no distinguishing features that boldly stand out to say "I'm a sandbar," this species is a close second to the dusky on the generic scale. Sandbars will vary in color from a bronze/gray to mostly gray and sport relatively large dorsal and pectoral fins. Like the dusky, sandbars are in the group of sharks classified as "large coastals" which signifies that they're more likely be found up on the Continental Shelf waters rather than out in the deeper water where the pelagic species are so common.

Sandbar sharks are a species that will often be caught in the surf and are known to frequently move up into coastal rivers and bays. In fact, the Delaware Bay is recognized as a nursery ground for this species, with the females entering the bay in early summer, giving birth, then heading back to sea, leaving the pups behind in an environment with less threat from predators.

In the South, sandbars are available all year but they don't start filtering in to the northern latitudes until water temperatures climb a little above the 60-degree mark. The first sandbars to arrive in the Mid-Atlantic region often do so around the first week of June and are mostly medium-size animals of 60 to 150 pounds. In mid to late July the nearshore waters start to fill up with smaller sand-bar sharks that might average 20 to 60 pounds. And in October and

The tall dorsal fin is a good identifier for a sandbar shark.

Sandbar sharks should al-ways be released.

early November the catch consists primarily of very small (less than 10 pound) sandbars that have just left their inshore nursery grounds and are headed south for the winter.

Like most sharks sandbars are caught at all depths, but they're more likely to be hooked up on baits positioned at or close to the bottom. Like the dusky, sandbars have a pretty large mouth and aren't shy about doing whatever they have to do to get even a big bait swallowed. So whenever anglers figure there's a chance sandbars might be in the area, it's always good to send a healthy-size bait like a bluefish head or whole bonito down to the bottom. Such baits are durable enough to withstand attacks by crabs and skates and still be attractive to a sandbar shark after a couple hours of soak-time.

Sandbar sharks are bulldog-like fighters that will always start the show with a few long runs and then settle in to a strong steady pull towards the bottom. If you were to compare the runs and jumps of a mako to that of a billfish, then you could say that a sandbar fights more like a tuna. Compared to other sharks the sandbar is more of a gentleman at boat-side and rarely makes the tagging and releasing process much of an ordeal.

Sandbar shark populations have been decimated after decades of being ruthlessly overfished by commercial fishermen for their meat and fins. Regulations are working to correct this tragedy, but considering the biology and slow reproductive capacity of this species it will take many more decades to rebuild the sandbar populations than it did to destroy them. The quality of sandbar meat is quite low and this species should always be released.

Dusky or Sandbar?

For years a big source of confusion for anglers has been trying to tell difference between a dusky and a sandbar shark. Since few anglers have the chance to view the two species side-by-side and memorize the subtle differences between species, it can be a tough identification to make when the boat's rolling, the shark's pulling, and the fisherman just wants to get the darn thing released so they can get the lines out and catch another! But since shark fishermen often encounter a lot of sandbar and dusky sharks, they really

Duskies are strong fighters that might be encountered in the near-shore or offshore waters.

The "generic" Dusky shark.

It may be small now, but if given a chance this little dusky could someday grow to be 12 feet long.

should know what they're catching, particularly if they get involved with tagging.

The most definitive trait that distinguishes duskies from sandbars is the location of the first dorsal fin. On a sandbar shark if you were to draw a line from where the front edge of the dorsal fin connects to the body, straight down the side of the shark to the belly, it would hit about the middle of the pectoral fin. Do the same to a dusky shark and the line would miss or just barely touch the very back edge of the pectoral fin. Also, a sandbar's first dorsal fin is proportionately much larger than that on a dusky, and a sandbar typically has a greater girth up in the shoulder area.

Color is not usually a good thing to use for identification because within a species the color of individual animals can vary a bit. But usually duskies tend to be more of a dark brown in color while sandbars will be gray or a gray/bronze. These color schemes tend to make the sandbar overall much lighter in color than the dusky, and when the angler finally starts to get the shark close to the boat the sandbar will appear gray and will be visible from the boat at a greater depth than the darker dusky.

Up close, anglers might sometimes notice clusters of little pea-size scars on the backs of duskies from the back of their first dorsal to the base of the tail. Most duskies will exhibit these scars but we seldom see them on sandbar sharks. Finally, the skin is very different between the two species. A dusky is covered by minutely small and sharp overlapping dermal denticles and a thin layer of slime. Run a hand from head to tail down a dusky and it will feel slimy and very smooth, go the other way and it will be slimy but very rough. Do the same with a sandbar shark and the shark will feel course in either

Dusky on the left, sandbar on the right – the subtle differences between these species can cause identification problems for anglers.

A mature sandbar shark, tagged and ready for release.

direction and there will be no slime because their skin consists of blunt, non-overlapping denticles, and no layer of slime.

Great White *(Carcharodon carcharias)*

There's not much I can possibly say about great white sharks that hasn't already be published, aired in hundreds of documentaries, or of course made into a movie. I'd wish I could claim to be an authority on the species, but in more than 30 years of sharking I've only had the opportunity to examine five dead ones (all brought in by other anglers) and encounter two offshore, one of which we tagged and released, and the other we watched (with no intention to drop it

Great whites are a protected species that are just as intriguing to observe
as they are to catch.

a bait) for 45 minutes as it swam behind the boat. I've also had the opportunity to interview a lot of anglers who have either caught, or encountered great whites while fishing.

I guess from my own limited experience I can say a few things that might shed a different light on this rather famous shark. First, anglers have to keep in mind that great whites are (rightfully) a prohibited species, so they're protected from being killed. This in itself should be a wake-up call for anyone who thinks they might want to drop a bait down into the maw of one of these monsters. Like when we had the 14-footer swim up to the back of my boat at 4:30 in the afternoon – sure I would have loved to hook my charter client up to the fish, and get it to the boat for some good photos and a tagging. But with a shark that size (1000 pounds? 2000? Who knows?) I knew that we wouldn't have it to the boat until well after dark, we couldn't bring it home (wouldn't want to anyway), and we wouldn't have been able to get any decent photos of it in the dark. It's dangerous enough dealing with any kind of fish of that size during the day, and in the dark a crew had darn-well better have their act together – or some of the stuff they've made movies about can really happen!

With only three of us on the boat that afternoon I assessed that we were seriously out of time and under manned, and so not wanting our encounter to end in any injuries to man or beast, I figured that the best thing we could do was to keep the lines out of the water and let the big guy just do his thing!

Well, okay... I tied a few baits onto a cord and tossed it over in an attempt to draw the shark closer for better photos, but overall we were happy just to watch the huge animal work a big circle through our chumline. And that's the kind of decisions fishermen have to be ready to make, because anytime someone drops a bucket of chum overboard they never know if something huge will come a-calling. That day we were less than five miles out and targeting small duskies and sandbars on light tackle when the white showed up. Like I said – you never know.

And that's something else anglers should know about great whites: it may be a little scary to think about but these are not exclusively deep-water sharks. While it's true that off the East Coast they're not very abundant in the first place, and when they are found, they're typically a comfortable distance offshore; they're also a species that will come into the nearshore waters if they have a reason. The big white that we watched and the "little" six and a half footer that we released were both encountered while we were fishing for small sharks within five miles of the coast.

As for their fighting abilities, the small one (we estimated 150 pounds) we caught was hooked up on 50 pound tackle and fought okay, but certainly not as hard or as well as a comparable size mako or hammerhead. Other anglers I've spoken with have mentioned the same thing; that pound for pound the white sharks they caught weren't extremely hard fighters. However, all of those sharks were under 500 pounds. Certainly a big white of a thousand pounds (or a few thousand pounds!) wouldn't even have to fight much, all it would have to do is stop swimming and its dead weight alone would be enough to best most anglers.

Hammerheads (Scalloped, Smooth, Great, and Bonnethead)

Proper shark identification may be a big problem for a lot of anglers, but when it comes to hammerheads even non-fishermen should be able to come close to hitting the nail on the head (excuse the pun) every time. I say "come close" because if someone simply sees a shark with a wing-like head and calls it a "hammerhead," they've only succeeded in narrowing the search down to sharks of the genus "Sphyrna" (from the Greek word meaning "hammer") but they still haven't identified the exact species. East and Gulf Coast anglers have four species of hammerheads they might encounter, and while all sport that handsomely unique head, much of the similarity stops right there. And anyone who wants to grow-up to be a great "Sphyrna" fisherman is going to have to know the difference between the species!

But before looking at the difference, I should probably first point out some similarities between the scalloped, smooth, and great hammerheads. These are warm water sharks and anglers should not expect to encounter them if the water temperatures aren't at least in the 70's. While hammerheads are ideally designed for bottom feeding (which they do a lot of) they are absolutely suckers for baits

Great whites are not common, but they could surprise any shark fisherman when they least expect it.

This small great white was docile and well mannered at the boat, certainly not the terror Hollywood makes the species out to be!

Using an ARC de-hooking tool to pop the hook out of a hammerhead.

----

fished right on the surface beneath a kite (for more about kite fishing for sharks see chapter eight). They also have a relatively small mouth and will take a small bait with much less hesitation than one which they might have to tear down to size. While it's always exciting to watch a hammerhead franticly rip up a big bait, since they'll often dislodge the hook in the process, it's not so good for catching the fish.

As long as they aren't overpowered with heavy tackle, hammerheads are incredible fighters. If a small one moves into the slick, anglers should quickly get the heavy stuff in and a light rod out. They won't jump, but hammerheads make some of the longest and strongest runs of any of the sharks. As strong as they are on the line, when brought to or in the boat they seem to burn out and die quicker than most sharks. Hammerheads destined for release should tagged, de-hooked, and turned loose as quickly as possible.

Watch that tail: anglers trying to get a tail rope around a decent size hammerhead will have an opportunity to find out what it's like to get slapped around with a two-by-six, and I can tell ya, it hurts! Want to impress your friends? If you're offshore and see a shark cruising on the surface way off in the distance, tell them it looks like a hammerhead. Then, if you're able to get close enough to actually see the head and identify the shark as a hammerhead your friends will think you have some kind of superhuman eyesight for being able to ID the shark from so far away. You don't have to tell them that most sharks seen cruising the surface are hammerheads and that you were just playing the odds.

Scalloped Hammerhead *(Sphyrna lewini)*

Until about the end of the 1990's the scalloped hammerhead was the most commonly caught hammerhead along much of the East Coast. On a single glassy-calm day in mid-summer we'd sometimes see dozens of these sharks spread out across the surface of the ocean, just cruising along with dorsal fins cutting a wake. They were decent size sharks too, usually 100 to 200 pounds. Unfortunately, intensive commercial fishing quickly and efficiently left its impression on populations of scalloped hammerheads and by the millennium encountering just one or two a season became a big deal.

Able to grow to about 12 feet long, scalloped hammerheads are not the largest sharks but they're certainly one of the largest of the hammerheads. Their color can vary from an olive to bronze/gray to all bronze. Like most hammerheads, this species is often seen swimming on the surface and by recognizing the tall and very erect dorsal fin a preliminary identification can often be made. Close to the boat this species can be positively identified by looking more closely at the dorsal fin and the head. The first dorsal fin of a great hammerhead is extra tall and the trailing edge of it curves back in a sickle-shape, while a scalloped hammerhead's dorsal fin is not quite as tall and the trailing edge has no backward curve. Looking at the leading edge of the head, a scalloped hammerhead has a slight depression or "scalloped-out" area directly in the center, while a smooth hammerhead does not.

Before they were overfished scalloped hammerheads of this size where a common catch. This photo is from the late 70's and is courtesy of Dale Timmons, of the *Coastal Fisherman*.

Scalloped hammerheads will venture out into deep waters, but they're usually encountered in the continental shelf waters. In the Mid-Atlantic we usually catch most of the larger ones in 10 to 30 fathoms, and juveniles in the nearshore waters. In more southern waters the larger scalloped hammerheads have a greater likelihood of being taken closer to shore.

Smooth Hammerhead *(Sphyrna zygaena)*

Smooth hammerheads are quite similar in size and characteristics as the scalloped, and they used to be caught less frequently than the scalloped, but since the scalloped has become so scarce their roles have been reversed along much of the East Coast. With a dark olive/gray color, in or out of the water this shark appears darker than the scalloped. The dorsal fin of the smooth is similar in shape to that of the scalloped but the center of the leading edge of the head is smooth, not indented as it is in the other hammerheads.

Great Hammerhead *(Sphyrna mokarran)*

Reaching lengths of over 18 feet and weights of over 1200 pounds, this species is the largest of the hammerheads. Because of its size and habit of moving into shallow water to feed on large prey, this is the species that's earned a bad reputation for hammerheads in general. While the other species don't deserve such a reputation, the great hammerhead is guilty as charged. This is a big, aggressive species that southern anglers are accustom to having attack and steal huge tarpon and other gamefish right off their hook.

Because great hammerheads are most likely to move into shallow water that's adjacent to very deep water, they are more likely to do so in the south – and they seem to have a taste for tarpon. Find concentrations of big tarpon in or near deep channels and you've probably found a good place for great hammerheads. From the Mid-Atlantic north this species is not a common catch because they tend to stay far offshore and out of range of most recreational shark fishermen.

Identification of this species is relatively simple as they are the only species of hammerhead that has such a tall and curved dorsal fin. The head of this shark is also unique in that it is rather straight, not curved back slightly like the other species.

Bonnethead *(Sphyrna tiburo)*

Bonnethead sharks are so different from other hammerheads that a lot of folks don't consider them to be in the same family. But despite their tiny size, they do have the hammer-ish head (more like a shovel actually) and most importantly they have that "Sphyrna" in their scientific name, so they must be considered hammerheads. Growing to maybe five feet, these are surely some of the smallest hammerheads caught by southern and Gulf Coast anglers. Catch one of these sharks over 20 pounds and you've got yourself a whopper! But don't let their small size fool you, these are vicious little sharks; lather yourself up with crab juice, lay on the bottom and they'll rip you to shreds. It might take a week but eventually they'll have you down to a skeleton.

All kidding aside, even though they're small, bonnetheads can be some of the most enjoyable sharks to pursue on light tackle. They're definitely a warm-water species that will rarely be taken north of the Carolinas. South Florida is prime territory for these sharks in the winter months and anglers who really want some fun should consider pursuing them over the shallow flats down in the Keys.
Bonnetheads will feed on a variety of small fish and mollusks but they have a strong taste for shrimp and crabs. Anglers who fish the flats will often find these sharks very plentiful (sometimes in less than two feet of water) and have the opportunity to sight-cast shrimp, crabs or even flies to them.

Shortfin Mako *(Isurus oxyrinchus)*

Most saltwater fishermen need no introduction to the mako shark. Many years ago when sharks in general were still considered nothing more than unwanted "trash-fish" that should be avoided at all expense, makos were heralded as gamefish worthy of pursuit and respect. And just by looking at these sharks it should be easy to see why.

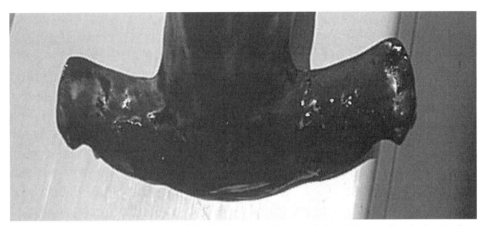

Smooth hammerheads are a bit darker in color and don't have the indentation in the center of their head as do the scalloped and the great.

The tall sickle-shaped dorsal identifies the great hammerhead.

Bonnethead sharks are a small species of hammerhead often found in very shallow water.

Makos have the profile of a cruise missile, and their habits and activities would indicate that the comparison is accurate for more than just their looks. Makos are fast, and deadly. Evolving into the speed machines that they are, they ended up with a sharply pointed nose that must easily slice through the water when they need to get somewhere quick. Behind their snout are two very large eyes that obviously belong to a hunter that relies much on its sight to help it navigate and find its prey in an environment of relatively clear water. Like other species in the "mackerel shark" family, the eyes of a mako appear totally black, as if the entire eyeball were a gigantic pupil. Of course this is not the case, but unless one gets uncomfortably close to a live mako's eye they'll never notice the other features behind the

Makos have always been one of the most popular targets of recreational shark anglers.

lens.

Behind and below the eyes a mako sports five gill openings that are proportionately larger than those found on most other species of shark. Makos need the larger gills to allow a higher volume of water to pass through and provide oxygen levels needed to sustain the mako's extreme energy level.

Working down the body and seeing the deep blue back, silvery sides, snow white belly, and firm, sleek, muscular build, it's easy to understand why makos are considered to be one of the most beautiful and fascinating sharks in the ocean. Just the tail alone is somewhat of an amazing feature. As is characteristic for members of the mackerel shark family (which also includes great whites, porbeagles, and salmon sharks) the base of the tail (known as the caudal peduncle) is very broad, but flat, and ends in structures known as "caudal keels" that project out from either side and help to stabilize and strengthen the tail.

Makos and other mackerel sharks have a "lunate" tail which means that, just like most other fish, the top and bottom lobes are much more similar in length than that of other sharks. It's this unique tail design that allows makos to demonstrate the speed and power that they do.

One of the most recognizable features of a mako is its smile. Even with its mouth shut tight, a number of this shark's chompers are always visible around the gum line. Mako teeth are long and thin dagger-like affairs that are not only extremely sharp at the tips, but also down either side — and there are a lot of them! A mako's teeth are not serrated like most other sharks but like a mouthful of double-edged knifes they have little trouble slicing though just about anything that passes between the jaws.

The average growth rate of makos is 50 to 60 pounds a year. Male makos reach sexual maturity somewhere around 100 to 125 pounds, but females aren't ready until they're over 500 pounds. Makos are ovoviviparous so their offspring are born alive. The pups are a little better than two feet long at birth and come out as carbon copies of mom and dad. Over the years we've caught a few of these little fellows under ten pounds, but every one had an attitude and was bold enough to take baits that were about as large as they were;

one attacked a large tuna head three times its own size, and another swam off after we released it but returned a minute later to bite the boat – no wonder mom leaves her pups to fend for themselves.

Makos are actually warm-blooded in that they can maintain a body temperature slightly higher than the surrounding water, a trait that certainly contributes to their ability to put on a good show when hooked on rod and reel. While makos seem to tolerate cooler water than many species of sharks such as tigers, hammerheads, and blacktips, they still tend to stick to the warmer waters, and anglers will seldom find them in temperatures much below 60 degrees.

As long as I can remember there has been a misconception by fishermen in the Mid-Atlantic region about the relationship between makos and water temperatures. In this area we typically start

Large gills allow makos to maintain high energy levels.

catching makos along the 20 fathom line in late May, when the water temperatures start to approach the 60 degree mark. This also coincides with the spring northern migration of big bluefish. As soon as the waters along the 20 fathom line warm up to a tolerable level, the makos move in from the deeper waters to partake of the bluefish —which just happens to be their primary prey in the Western Atlantic.

As long as good numbers of bluefish remain concentrated along the 20 fathom line so will the makos. But usually by the beginning of July the bluefish start to thin out. Without a primary food source to hold them in the area, the makos also disperse. They don't necessarily leave the entire area, they just don't stay congregated along the 20 fathom line and are, therefore, more difficult for anglers

A mako's tooth and jaw design is ideal for snagging and shredding prey of all sizes.

to target. By then the water temperatures are pushing into the lower 70's which has caused a lot of fishermen to mistakenly conclude that the makos leave to migrate north because the local waters have become too warm. Wrong! Anyone who thinks that 70-something degree water is too warm for makos might be interested to know that these fish are regularly caught in the tropics, where water temperatures never drop below that level. Sure, it can be too cold for makos or other sharks, but rarely will it be too warm.

With makos being more of an open water species, it's rare to find them too close to shore or in very shallow water. However, it does happen. We've hooked a few of them within five miles of Maryland's coast, and I know of at least one that was taken in the shallow backcountry waters of the Florida Keys. Except for situations such as I previously described (where makos move inshore to the 20 fathom line to feed on bluefish), in many cases anglers will probably need to fish close to the edge of the continental shelf to find clear water and a better than average shot at encountering a mako.

Sport fishermen have taken makos in excess of 1,200 pounds, but along the East Coast and in the Gulf of Mexico makos over 500 pounds are exceptional catches. Most recreational anglers will encounter makos that range in size from 30 to 300 pounds. Smaller makos are more likely to move inshore while the bigger ones tend to stay out beyond the shelf waters, but both sizes can show-up anywhere at any time. One August morning we were fishing three miles off Ocean City Maryland, and having a lot of light tackle fun with four foot dusky and sandbar sharks. We couldn't understand why the last three sharks gave us a brief fight and then broke off, until a 500 pound mako swam up to the back of the boat. Apparently, the big guy was snacking on our smaller sharks. Needless to say we switched from light to heavy tackle really quickly! The big mako took our bait five feet off the transom, and we actually had to move the boat away from the fish before we could set the hook. That was certainly an unexpected size and species of shark to encounter just three miles out, but it demonstrates the point that sharks will leave their normal haunts when a good food source is available – in this case that food was small sharks.

When it comes to targeting makos there's no need to depart

Bluefish like this are common visitors to shark fishermen's chum lines and they give makos a reason to be there too.

Makos start life at less than ten pounds but grow 50 to 60 pounds a year. Small ones like this are fun on light tackle but must be released.

from the general shark fishing tactics as I describe in the Techniques chapter of this book. Makos are just sharks; put out a good spread of baits for the rest of the gang and if a mako wanders up your chum line he'll take what you're offering. However, one thing to keep in mind with makos is that they'll typically take a bite-size bait more quickly than a mouthful. Even if you hope to hook a 1,000-pounder I wouldn't suggest fishing a huge tuna head or any other bait that the shark can't easily slurp down. While makos will usually be hooked on baits close to the surface, anglers would be mistaken to consider them to be surface feeders. These sharks will feed at all depths and over the years we've hooked a lot of makos on baits fished close to the bottom.

Maybe more so than other sharks, makos will sometimes circle a bait for a long time before deciding whether or not to eat it. Particularly when fishing in areas where we anticipate makos, I like to periodically crank each bait at least half-way back to the boat before letting it drift back out to its original position. I don't know if it's the extra movement of the bait, or the thought that their lunch might be getting away from them, that will often prompt a hesitant mako to hit a bait that's being cranked in. With this in mind, at the end of the day anglers should pay particular attention when retrieving their baits for the trip home. We once went all day without a bite, but as I was cranking in the last bait a dark fin popped up behind it. That fin was attached to a 225 pound mako that pretty much saved the day for us.

Makos are often described as the best fighting of all the sharks. While I agree that (pound for pound) it would be tough to find a shark that fights any better than a mako, when I think about spinners, hammerheads, threshers, blacktips and a few other species, I'm convinced that most of the top contenders will put up a fight that's at least as good. Makos, however, do have one advantage—they can launch out of the water like a missile from a submarine. And that's probably the best way to describe it, too. They don't jump like other fish, but makos typically launch straight up five or ten feet with no problem. Some people will say they'll go twice that height. I might have seen 15 feet, but I think a 20 foot launch is a bit of a stretch. Anyway, whatever altitude they reach it's always impressive —very

Large makos like this 684-pounder may be a once in a lifetime catch, but when they get this size their meat tends to get tough and loses much of the popular mako flavor, so anglers must decide for themselves if boating such a shark is the ethical thing to do.

impressive!

But just like any other fish, not every mako will grace the crew of a boat with a demonstration of its jumping ability. Probably less than half will go airborne, but when they do it will usually be either immediately after the hook is set, or during a fast run. Crew members can often get good photos of a mako in the air by keeping close to the angler during the fight and being focused and ready to snap the shot just as soon as they see that the shark is making a fast run. Since makos tend to jump vertically more so than horizontally, there will be just enough "hang-time" at the apex of the jump to click an exciting photo.

We once hooked a mako that put up absolutely no fight as it allowed the angler to crank it directly to the boat. We just knew that as soon as we grabbed the leader the shark would get the message and give us a few runs, but it never happened. Even after we gaffed the shark, it just laid there as calm as could be. It wasn't until we actually tried to put the mako in the boat that it finally went absolutely ballistic – the darn thing tricked us! The point of that story is to show that, despite the mako's well-deserved reputation as an awesome fighting machine, sometimes they just don't give a good account of their abilities. But just because they don't fight doesn't mean they can't. Many times we've had makos come to the boat after just a few minute battle, but as soon as we grab the leader or plant the tag they take off on a run and can't be brought back to the boat for another hour or more. If they come in too quickly that might just mean they're saving their energy for an opportune time to explode.

Longfin Mako *(Isurus paucus)*

Because longfin makos typically stay out in the deeper waters beyond the continental shelf and are apparently not as abundant as the shortfin mako, recreational anglers seldom encounter this species of shark. However, I've often been questioned by anglers who were not sure if what they caught was a longfin or a shortfin. Considering that at this time the longfin mako is on the NMFS Prohibited Species List and is, therefore, protected from harvest, I figure it's probably prudent to at least mention some obvious differences between the two.

The mouth area of a longfin mako is a dirty-gray to almost black.

Most of the time anglers think that maybe they have caught a longfin because the mako they are looking at beside the boat has longer than normal looking pectoral fins. To this I can only say that on every longfin I've ever seen these fins didn't just appear to maybe be a little longer than usual – they were much longer. So much longer, in fact, that there was no doubt I was looking at a longfin. So if there's a question at all, it's probably a shortfin.

Longfin mako lack the beautiful color scheme of the shortfin. Instead of silvery sides, the longfin's colors go from a deep dark blue (almost black) back to a dark gray on the sides and then a white underside. However, the most distinguishing feature between the two species are the colors of the underside of the snout and lower jaw. On a shortfin this area is a vivid white in color while on the longfin it's a dark gray or almost black. So in most cases, unless anglers are fishing way out in the deep and catch an overall dark colored shark with obviously extra-long pectoral fins and a dirty face, it's probably not a longfin mako.

Sand Tiger *(Carcharias Taurus)*

I guess that every family has a member or two that's...well... a little on the homely side. The shark family has its beautiful makos, the sleek handsome spinners, and the illustrious threshers – then there's the sand tiger. I don't want to sound cruel, but sand tigers are surely one of the ugliest sharks in the ocean. With their little pig-like eyes, rough brown/gray blotchy skin, short little fins, and long thin teeth that stick out and can be seen even when its cavernous jaws

Sand tigers might not be the prettiest sharks in the sea.

are closed, this is one hideous critter.

Of course, anglers know that looks aren't everything. There are lot of fish that aren't too pretty to look at but still get the nod from fishermen because they put up a nice scrap. Unfortunately, Mr. Sand Tiger loses on that one, too. They can do a good job of throwing their weight around, but as far as the struggle goes, it's like hooking into the proverbial sack of rocks.

But all that's not to say that these aren't incredible sharks. After all, who ever said that a fish has to be pretty and conform to some kind of sport fishing standard to be considered as an amazing member of the ocean's ecosystem? They're ugly as sin and don't fight much, but sand tiger sharks are actually one of the coolest sharks a fisherman can encounter.

The long thin teeth of the sand tiger are best suited for snagging relatively small fish.

Sand tigers are nearshore sharks that are seldom encountered in the deep waters too far from shore. In the winter months
they're found from the Carolinas south, but in the summer they'll
extend their range as far north as the Gulf of Maine. Sand tigers will
congregate (sometimes in large numbers) over and around wrecks,
reefs, and shoals that hold an adequate supply of bait and these are
the areas where most anglers will encounter them.

The habits, biology, and fierce-look of these sharks make
them ideal for display in large public aquariums. Despite their outward appearance, sand tigers are a relatively docile shark that feeds
primarily on small fish, rays, and crustaceans. These sharks are
ovoviviparous, so instead of an umbilical cord the developing young
are nourished by a yolk sack. The embryos are also "oviphagous,"

Large eyes are not always important in the often murky waters frequented
by the sand tiger.

which means they cannibalize their smaller offspring while still inside their mother. Eventually each of the two oviducts contain only one pup which are about three feet long when born.

It's well known that since sharks lack the gas-filled air bladder found in most other fishes, if they don't keep swimming forward they will descend to the bottom in the same way that an airplane will glide to the earth if its propeller quits turning. An amazing characteristic of sand tigers is their ability to attain neutral buoyancy underwater. For the same reason scuba divers will inflate or deflate their buoyancy compensators with air to so that they can effectively hover at one depth, sand tigers will actually come to the surface of the water and gulp air, which they are able to retain in their stomach. When they swim back to the depths the trapped air helps them to stay at desired depths with very little forward movement or kicking of their tails.

When a fisherman hooks a sand tiger the fight will typically involve a couple of short slow runs of less than 50 yards and then the shark will stubbornly hold mostly straight down and below the boat. Even on 50 pound tackle it will be a workout to pump the shark up when it wants to stay down. The nature of the struggle, and the fact that the shark probably took a bait off the bottom, might have the angler wondering if they didn't hook a large ray. Watch for the bubbles – as the shark struggles to stay down it will eventually release the air in its stomach. Seeing these bubbles is a sure-fire way to tell what's on the end of the line.

After the shark is released it will immediately swim back to the depths, but then it has a problem; it expelled all its air during the fight and now it can't hover. If anglers watch the waters around the boat for the first few minutes after the release, they'll often see the same shark return to the surface, take a big gulp of air, and then thrash its tail in the air as it struggles to get back down. Like I said – these are pretty cool sharks!

The fact that sand tigers congregate in large groups and produce only two pups every couple years makes this species very susceptible to being overfished, and that's exactly what happened. By the mid 90's populations of sand tigers had been decimated so badly that in many areas where they were once very common they became virtually non-existent. Government regulations finally put a stop to the slaughter when sand tigers became one of the first sharks to be placed on the Prohibited Species List. Since then their numbers appear to be creeping back up, but do to their very slow reproductive cycle it'll likely take a long time before this can be considered a "recovered" species.

Even though proper release methods usually result in little or no harm to a shark, a small percentage of post-release mortality is inevitable in any fishery. If too much fishing pressure occurs on the same group of sharks, the odds for negative impact even from catch-and-release will certainly increase. Recreational anglers must do their part to help assist the recovery of sand tiger sharks by not engaging them too frequently. They might be ugly slugs, but these fascinating sharks need and deserve all the respect and protection they can get.

Thresher *(Alopias vulpinus)*

There are actually two species of thresher shark anglers might encounter along the East Coast and Gulf of Mexico, they include the common thresher (Alopias vulpinus) and the bigeye thresher (Alopias superciliosus). Of the two, the bigeye is seldom taken by recreational anglers as it's apparently not as abundant and it frequents the deeper waters beyond the continental shelf. However, the common thresher is a shark encountered regularly by fishermen in the Mid-Atlantic and Northeast and occasionally in the south.

It's tough to imagine a better shark to suit the needs of recreational anglers than the common thresher. Threshers will put up as powerful and exciting a fight as any of the other sharks, including long runs, jumps, and a variety of other tactics that will keep fishermen in awe. Depending upon the location, time of year, and availability of bait, threshers might be found anywhere from the surf-line all the way out to the 100 fathom line. And even though threshers will grow to over 700 pounds, smaller animals are encountered frequently enough that they can also provide anglers with excellent light-tackle opportunities. Although they're usually taken by conventional shark fishing tactics, threshers (like makos) are a species that will sometimes be accidentally hooked by anglers trolling for other

The small mouth and teeth of a thresher indicate a shark that feeds primarily on small prey.

There's no mistaking what you're looking at when you see the long tail of a thresher.

fish.

You don't have to be a shark expert to take one look at a thresher and realize that it's unique among sharks. The colors are a stunning combination of blue, purple, silver, and white, and the top lobe of the thresher's tail is as long as the entire body of the fish itself. But the tail is not just designed for propulsion, it's an effective tool used to whack and stun the small schooling fish these sharks primarily feed on. An inspection of the other end of this fish reveals a very small mouth with tiny teeth clearly indicating that, despite their potentially large size, threshers are designed to feed on very small prey.

Anglers should remember these characteristics when fishing for threshers and keep their baits small and their leaders long. How long? A 400 pound thresher is going to have a body that's seven to eight feet in length, double that for the tail and you've got animal that

A big thresher can be more than 16 feet long.

might be 16 feet long. That makes for a long leader if you want to keep the line from contacting the shark.

We've hooked threshers on surface baits presented under kites, on float baits, and in the mid-range, but most of our thresher bites typically come on baits fished close to the bottom. But anglers should know that just because they hook a thresher on the bottom doesn't mean that they won't be seeing the shark up on the surface very soon. It's not uncommon for these sharks to pick up a deep bait, and before the hook is even set come racing to the surface and jump. Needless to say, such actions can surprise a crew and cause more than just a little commotion on deck.

To find threshers, anglers should look for areas where small schooling type fish such as mackerel, herring, and menhaden are congregated and fish close to, or among, the schools. In the Mid-Atlantic region anglers typically hook 200 to 500 pound threshers in late May and early June in 15 to 25 fathoms of water and then in late summer and fall find juvenile, 20 to 100 pound, threshers within 10 miles of the beach.

In recent years it has been observed that many if not most of the large female thresher sharks taken in the Mid-Atlantic region in late May and early June are gravid (pregnant) with four to six very well developed pups. With so much still unknown about the biology of threshers, and the health and future of their populations, one can only assume that harvesting gravid females cold have catastrophic results on the future of this species. By adopting a policy to release all female threshers caught before July 1st anglers will at least give these incredible sharks a better chance to deliver their pups and per-petuate their species.

Tiger *(Geleocerdo cuvier)*

Great whites can grow larger, but of all the species the aver-age shark fisherman is likely to catch, tigers are the largest. Recre-ational anglers have landed tigers over 1700 pounds, and given the opportunity, this species can reach more than a ton. That's a lot of fish, and a good reason to keep the light tackle stowed in the cabin when a big tiger is in the chum line.

Tigers are warm-water sharks that may be found in any of the nearshore or offshore waters along the entire East Coast and Gulf of Mexico (not to mention the rest of the world) as long as they have temperatures of 70 degrees or better. Like most species, large tigers will typically tend to stay farther out in the deeper water while the juveniles will more likely be the ones encountered closer to shore. Besides their blotches and stripe-like markings, tigers are characterized by a huge head and shoulder area followed by a sharply tapering back half. The front end of these sharks is so large that from above they almost resemble gigantic tadpoles.

A tiger shark's unique markings make it easy to identify.

The huge jaw and unique tooth design of the tiger allow this species to eat darn near anything it wants.

The big head holds an exceptionally large jaw adorned with a set of unique serrated teeth that hook sharply to the side. This tooth design allows tiger sharks to feed on sea turtles (a favorite prey) and actually crush through the shells without breaking their teeth in the process. Tigers are probably the species that years ago prompted someone to label sharks "the ocean's garbage collectors." Stomach contents of these sharks have revealed enough animate and inanimate objects to show that they don't always show much discretion in what they eat–no wonder they get so fat!

Big tigers are going to be on the lookout for big prey, so fishermen will want to focus their efforts in areas where there are good numbers of turtles or large fish such as tuna, jacks, rays, or other sharks. We once hooked a 350 pound tiger on a four inch bait intended for bluefish, but anglers targeting these sharks will do best if they use large, fresh baits that have a lot of "scent-appeal" such as tuna heads, rays, whole bonito or false albacore.

Tigers were once a common catch in the Mid-Atlantic and Northeast, but like so many other shark species, their number have slipped dramatically. They're still occasionally taken in the northern latitudes, but these days the Southeast and Gulf provide anglers the best opportunity to encounter tiger sharks. The poor quality and taste

The sheer weight alone of big tigers can make them a handful, but they'll usually calm down quickly beside the boat, and allow for a quick photo and safe release.

of tiger shark meat makes this species of no use for food, therefore, there is absolutely no reason why any recreational fisherman should do anything but catch-and-release this species.

Lemon Shark *(Negaprion brevirostris)*

The lemon shark is a very common year-round species in the waters that surround Florida and much of the Gulf. In the summer they'll extend their range as far north as the Carolinas. Even if they've never fished for sharks, most who have spent time on the shallow flats of the Florida Keys know the lemon shark because, besides the nurse and the bonnethead, they're one of the most common to see freely swimming about or sometimes laying on the bottom.

As their name implies these sharks will sometimes appear yellowish/green in color but they might also be more brown or gray. Lemon sharks will grow to over 10 feet and 400 pounds, however, most fishermen will encounter animals at less than 200 pounds. In fact, the shallows are nursery areas for this species and anglers will

Lemon shark are often taken from small boats in shallow, tropical waters.

often find juveniles under 10 pounds swimming among the mangroves in less than two feet of water.

Pound for pound lemon sharks may not put up as much fight as the blacktips, bulls, spinners, or some of the other sharks they share the same waters with. However, anglers can still expect a decent battle from these fish and like most sharks, the lighter the tackle the better the fight. Some of the best fighters are not necessarily the largest. It's more likely to encounter small to medium size lemons in less than three feet of water, and at such shallow depths it seems the sharks have a lot more determination not to be brought to the boat. By anchoring their boat in a position so that the current takes the scent of their chum across the shallows to a deeper channel or cut, anglers can draw lemon sharks onto the flat and have a great time sight-casting to individual sharks as they come within range. Lemons are very opportunistic feeders that will take a variety of bait and can also be coxed into taking plugs, jigs, or even flies.

Basking *(Cetorhinus maximus)*

Okay friends, the only reason I'm mentioning anything about basking sharks is so that when anglers are out there fishing for other types of sharks and they encounter one of these giants that they know what they're looking at. Many years ago basking sharks used to be netted or harpooned commercially for their oil, but today they are a prohibited species. To feed, basking sharks swim with their huge mouths open and strain plankton from the water with their gill rakers. Since they eat plankton there's no sense in sport fishermen trying to catch them anyway–unless they have very, very small hooks!

Basking sharks are gray-brown in color and a notable characteristic is the five enormous gill slits that are so long they almost encircle the entire head. These sharks can grow to over 30 feet long and it's this huge size and their basic profile that often confuses anglers and has them thinking that they might be looking at a great white. To help fuel the misidentification, these sharks have a habit of swimming up on the surface where they are easily observed and will sometimes even make a few curious circles around a boatload of shark fishermen.

CHAPTER 4

Chumming

This is a long chapter, not because I particularly like talking about blood and guts, but because I consider proper chumming techniques to be the most important aspect of catching sharks. After all, if you can't get them around the boat, you certainly don't need to worry about hooks, baits, gaffs, tags, or anything else that goes along with actually catching a shark. After so many years of standing over a chumline I've come to know that there's a whole lot more to "getting it right" than simply tossing a bucket or bag of chum over the side then sitting back and waiting for the sharks to bite. Oh how I wish that it could be that easy!

The first time I went fishing specifically for sharks, I was 15 and didn't have clue what I was doing. Of course that was 1973, and at the time it was next to impossible to find any kind of information about recreational shark fishing. So my friends and I pooled our limited knowledge and resources and came up with a plan. Our bait and tackle consisted of a dozen flounder heads, two spinning rods, and for chum we had a couple paper grocery bags filled with leftover table-scraps that a few neighbors agreed to save for us. Instead of running my friend's 18 foot boat up the bay to go water-skiing (like we told his father we were going to do) we headed out of the Ocean City inlet bound for big adventure with monster sharks!

Our plan was simple: go into the ocean, put out chum, and catch big sharks. After running a whole mile offshore we figured we were out far enough, so we shut down and started our drift. After two flounder heads were impaled on hooks and cast from the boat we went about laying our chum line. Our chumming technique was as basic as the rest of our plan—dump one bag of table scraps over, then the other, and wait for the sharks to come in.

While the sharks didn't exactly come rushing in, we all agreed that we learned some valuable lessons about chumming that day. No sooner did the chum hit the water before we knew that chicken and steak bones sink, as do green beans and potato peels. However, corncobs, lettuce, and dinner rolls float nicely and give a good indication which way the rest of the chum is drifting. Before the trip was over we actually did catch two or three small dusky sharks, although somehow I doubt our chum had much to do with it.

Chumming is probably one of the most misunderstood aspects of shark fishing. On one side we have Hollywood movies trying to convince us that a little trickle of blood from a scratched leg will have sharks zooming in from miles away, on the other we have tournament shark fishermen using 55 gallons of chopped up fish and glop to chum in a couple blue sharks. Somewhere between those two extremes is the proper technique for fishermen to attract sharks to their baits. But before I go any further let me clarify one thing: there is no one universal method that will attract any species of shark in any location. Tactics that work for lemon and bull sharks in the Florida Keys will not necessarily work to attract makos and blue sharks in northeast canyons. But there are common principals and techniques that all sharkers should know and keep in mind when trying to draw in sharks.

That Amazing Sense of Smell!

Like a hungry neighbor honing in on your backyard barbeque grill, sharks use their well-developed olfactory system to follow their noses to the source of familiar smells they recognize as food. Sharks can detect very minute bits of scent in the water, and many species are content to travel long distances to find the source of the smell. In the same way a good breeze might carry the smell of your sizzling steaks to the end of your street, with a good current the scent of fish can travel a long way in the ocean. But despite the hype that would have many believing that the smell of food brings sharks rushing in from all angles, fishermen must recognize that sharks must be down-current of an object if they are going to smell it. Think again about that barbeque grill; it can be putting out some mighty fine aroma, but you'd never know it if you're upwind—maybe that's why only half of your neighbors drop by when you're having a cookout!

A shark's nose is its long-range prey detector.

Current Carries the Chum

With this in mind, it should make sense that shark fishermen would want to keep a very close watch on the direction of the current. Particularly when choosing a location to set up and fish from, no matter if their boat will be drifting or anchored, anglers should always consider three things: 1) where the sharks should be in relation to bottom contours, wrecks, reefs, shoals, etc.; 2) which direction the current will take the chum; and 3) Where the boat must be so that the chum will flow across the area where the sharks should be holding.

To better understand where a chumline goes as it leaves their boat, anglers must first consider a few basics about ocean currents. Despite what it may appear from the deck of a boat, currents do not necessarily follow the wind. A sustained wind may push the first couple feet of the ocean's surface in the direction the wind is heading, but below that depth the true current might be heading in an entirely different direction, and this is the current that will dictate where the chum will ultimately go. Anglers should also know that, depending upon where they are fishing, currents may or may not be directly affected by tidal flows. So, if a current is not flowing in a direction favorable to their fishing efforts, there's no guarantee it'll change directions within the next six hours.

From a Drifting Boat

The direction the boat travels will most likely be a result of the wind–not the current. Even if the boat is drifting to the northeast, the current could actually be heading directly to the west, east, or any other point on the compass, and to confuse things even more, the chum will be flowing from the boat in the same direction as the current.

As complicated as this may sound it's really not hard to make sense of. Simply mark the boat's position on a chart, draw an arrow through it that represents the direction of the wind (and therefore the boat), then draw three or four perpendicular lines from the wind line out in the direction the current is heading. These lines will indicate which way the chum is actually heading as it leaves the boat, and from which direction the sharks will be coming from.

By plotting the boat and the chum's travel paths in this fashion, anglers should be able to properly choose starting points for their drift that will allow the chum to properly flow to areas where the anglers feel will most likely be holding sharks.

From an Anchored Boat

Shark fishermen who anchor need to know which way the current is flowing so they can position the boat so that their chum will flow to the desired location. Because the current could be running to any point around the compass, just because an anchored boat points into the wind doesn't mean that the current is flowing back behind the vessel. Surface current generated by the wind might pull float-lines with them, but deep lines will always "go with the flow" of the actual current. So if they aren't sure of the direction of the current when they first shut down, anglers will certainly find out just as soon as they put their deep line(s) in the water. If it's determined that the current is running the wrong way anglers should haul in all of their gear, pull up the anchor, and then re-drop it in a position that's truly up-current of the area they want their chumline to run through.

Power Chumming

Rather than waiting for drift or current to stretch their chumline out from the boat, anglers sometimes choose to give their chum a little jump-start by "power chumming" before they shut down to drift or anchor. This process simply involves chumming while the boat is still moving and may be initiated as close to or as far away from where they're actually going to fish as the anglers choose, but usually a distance of one half to one mile is about right.

Power chumming requires a faster than usual flow of chum, and can be done while the boat is still running at cruising speed, although it's more controllable when the vessel is slowed to a pace of about six knots. But even at that speed, tying the chum bucket off the transom and letting it beat around in the prop-wash will create unnecessary problems.

The best way to deploy the chum is by leaving the bucket on the deck and pumping water into it with a saltwater wash-down hose through one of the holes in the lid. The rate of chum can be controlled by adjusting the flow of the wash-down pump or by increasing or decreasing the hole-size in the bucket's lid. If the bucket is left close to a deck scupper the chum will wash out of the bucket and then directly overboard. If the boat isn't fitted with scuppers that allow this, the bucket can be set on a swim platform or hung over the side by the handle. Power chumming can quickly burn up a lot of chum so anglers who figure to use this method should plan ahead and bring extra rations.

Blood Will Bring Them In – Won't It?

Sharks love blood, right? According to Hollywood they do. Even the documentaries like to point out that sharks can smell one part blood in a million parts of water. Well that sounds impressive, but lets face it, there's a heck of a lot more than a million parts of water out there, and a shark is going to smell what it smells, and no matter if it's blood, urine, scales, fins, tails, or fish farts, it's all going to tell them that there may be a potential meal up ahead. Whether or not the shark chooses to follow it to the source will likely depend upon how hungry it is and how strongly the shark associates the smell with food.

Back to blood. While I'm no biochemist, I'll go out on a limb by saying that blood does nothing more to attract a shark other than carry to it the scent of the critter that did the bleeding. Okay, nothing wrong with that, the idea of chumming is to tell the sharks that there's something up-current that they should come and check out. The problem with using blood for chum is the actual process of using it. If you've ever tried to lay out a nice consistent trail of blood you'll discover something that you already know–blood clots! So if you

Give a nurse shark what it wants and you can have it nipping at your outboard!

think you're going to punch a hole in that can of blood and simply let it trickle out over the course of the day, forget it, because in no time the opening will be clogged-up and you'll be wiggling a screwdriver in the hole trying to get it flowing again. That won't work so you'll punch another hole, but that'll clog just like the first one did. After your third hole meets with similar results you'll pop the lid off the bucket and start ladling. Now everyone aboard will enjoy wonderful aroma of the foul-smelling stuff that lies inside and which has also begun to turn to the consistency of a runny pudding. At this point, anyone not left gagging by the stench need only look inside the bucket to appreciate the true horror of what resides inside and find reason not to ever use blood as chum again!

How do I know all this? Let's just say that back during my own "infant years" of shark fishing I did a lot of experimenting with different types of chum, and I took advantage of a couple opportunities to try both beef and chicken blood. Despite all of the inherent hassles, if blood proved to be effective at attracting sharks, I'd still be using it. But I learned my lesson early and have no desire to go through that again!

Give'em What They Know – Fish!

Show me a bunch of sharks that routinely feed on pork, beef, or poultry, and I'll concede that chum made from those critters might be worth using. But the fact is, we want to spend our time catching sharks, not trying to educate them that if they follow our scent trail of bacon bits and goose guts it'll lead them to a wonderful smorgasbord. While we all know that in some places around the world certain sharks habitually feed on seabirds, turtles, seals, whales, and dolphins, recreational shark anglers needn't even consider using any parts of those animals for bait or chum because all of them are either endangered or protected and, therefore, possession of them or even their parts is illegal. Besides that, the sharks most East Coast and Gulf anglers pursue will not likely be feeding on such animals and so they wouldn't provide a quality bait or chum in the first place. If they want to catch a shark anglers need to give'em what they want, give'em what they know, give'em FISH!

Having established that fish should be our first choice for chum we still have the dilemma of what kind of fish to use. Often that decision is out of our hands because we're limited to the type of chum they sell in our local tackle shops, or whatever kind of fish we can buy, catch, or get from the local fish cleaning station.

Of all these options, I usually consider the cleaning station to be the best place to acquire fish for chum, and it's not just because those fish will usually be free for the taking. No cost is great but more importantly, fish brought in for cleaning will likely be good and fresh because they have been very recently caught and kept properly iced. They'll also represent local fish that the sharks are presently feeding on. I also feel a lot better about making chum out of parts and carcasses from fish brought in for human consumption than catching and killing a bunch of fish just for chum. It's a great way to make total use of the resource, it's kind of like recycling, and this can be of some benefit to marina personnel as well because whatever is taken away for chum is just that much less that they'll have to dispose of at the end of the day.

Types of Fish For Chum

During the early summer bluefish are the primary food source of makos off our Mid-Atlantic and northeast region, and sharkers spend a lot of time targeting this prized species. At times bluefish can be so abundant that anglers have no trouble catching a virtually unlimited supply of them, providing one of the few opportunities to actually match bait and chum to exactly what the sharks are feeding on.

But in most cases it's going to be difficult if not impossible to know if local sharks are feeding primarily on one food source, or as is more often the case, feeding on a variety of opportunities as they encounter them. Just because there's a lot of one type of fish in the area doesn't necessarily mean that's what the sharks are primarily targeting or even what they prefer to eat if given other options. In most cases the best anglers can do is to make an educated guess at what their local sharks will readily recognize as food, consider their own options as to what's available for chum, and then make a best-guess at what to use.

Members of the tuna fam-
ily: bonito, albacore, bluefin,
yellowfin, etc. all make some
of the best bait and chum for
sharks.

Almost any species of fish might work effectively as shark
chum. But some, such as bluefish, bonito, false albacore, herring,
menhaden, Atlantic mackerel, and tuna, have become quite well
known for their shark attracting qualities and, just as important, their
availability. Even if anglers are unable to catch them on their own,
some of these fish such as menhaden, herring, and mackerel can
be purchased frozen, or sometimes fresh, from local fish markets,
tackle shops, or directly from the commercial fishermen who catch
them.

An added bonus of acquiring a decent quantity of fish for
chum is the option of being able to sort through and pull out some of
the better fish for use as bait. Whether they'll be used soon or put in
the freezer for future trips, it's can be a great opportunity for anglers
to ensure that the next time they fish they'll have quality baits that
match their chum.

What's Best?

My own personal preference for the top five fish to be used for chum in the Mid-Atlantic area includes tuna, false albacore, bonito, mackerel, and bluefish–in that order. But right from the start I'll have to say that I have no good reason for ranking them that way other than that's just my personal liking, because even after more than 35 years of chumming with everything from lettuce to livers, I still haven't been able to prove that one type of chum works any better than another. How can you know? You go out one day and catch a bunch of sharks on one type of chum and the next day you try something else and catch nothing. Was it the chum? Or was it just that the sharks had moved out of the area? Or was it just a slow day of fishing? We're going to have good days and bad days even when we don't change chum types.

Maybe you noticed that menhaden, didn't even make my top-five list. Because menhaden are a very strong and oily fish that are caught in large quantities at a relatively low cost, it has become a very popular fish to process into chum. Menhaden chum (and bait) is effective on a wide variety of fish, including sharks, and I still use it on occasion, but since I really don't recall any outstanding results while using menhaden for shark chum, I've come to use it only when the other options are not available.

So given the choice, yea I'd go for the tuna first and work my way down the list if I had to. But if I can't get my first choice I won't spend my day pining for something different in my chum bucket, I'll still expect to catch sharks!

The Chumline

Chum is supposed to attract sharks to your baits, not feed them before they get there. Let me say that again. Chum is supposed to attract sharks to your baits, not feed them before they get there! I emphasize that point because it is so extremely important when it comes to catching sharks. It's also a principal that shark anglers often lose sight of in overzealous attempts to catch sharks by adopting a "more is better" approach to chumming. As I mentioned earlier, sharks smell their way to their next meal, and all they need is enough scent in the water to peak their interest and whet their appetite. If they're inclined to come, they'll come.

By clouding the water with a massive barrage of ground-up fish, fish parts, fish oil, blood, and any other meaty tidbit they can find slopping around the bottom of their fish box, anglers only succeed in creating a wide and confusing highway of smells and food that might not be so easy for a shark to follow directly to the boat.

To better appreciate the problem, anglers should try and visualize what's going on beneath the waves and down-current from their boat: as chum leaves the boat it disperses in a big cone-shape swath with fish oils staying up on the surface (producing a "sheen" on the water,) light, fatty particles of meat staying higher in the water column longer (because they sink more slowly,) and denser bits of chum sinking faster and eventually reaching the bottom first. The farther away from the boat, the wider the cone of chum becomes. Sharks and other fish that enter the cone at its wider section swim inside a huge cloud of smells and chunks of fish. Other fish of all sizes also swim about the cloud and feed on the bits and chunks. All this activity surely peaks a sharks interest but might not give it reason to follow the chum to its source and a fisherman's baits. Why should it? There are plenty of baitfish and free chunks floating right back to the shark, no need to leave food to find food!

Now let's consider a modest flow of ground-up fish steadily streaming all day from some guy's chum bucket. Again the lighter oils and fatty particles will tend to stay up while the heavier stuff sinks. But because the particles are more consistent in size they'll tend to be affected by the current more uniformly and, therefore, instead of a cone-shape, the spread of chum as it leaves the boat will be more of a vertical fan shape that won't be as wide, even though it will still cover the entire water column from top to bottom. The chum will still attract other types of fish and the smallest of those will be able to eat the chum, but larger fish and certainly the sharks will only find a promise of food at the end of the trail, not a free lunch along the way. If they want to eat they'll have to come all the way in. Remember, chum should attract–not feed!

So let's say we've managed to get hold of 50 pounds of mackerel for chum and we're ready to go sharking. How are we going to properly deploy these fish as chum in a manor that will bring sharks close to our boat, hungry enough to take our baits when they arrive? Should we smash them up and put them over the side in a burlap sack or mesh bag? Mince them up in a grinder or mechanical fish-chopper mounted to the side of the boat? Cut them up into little pieces, add water and ladle the "gruel" overboard one scoop at a time? The answers to those questions are no, no, and definitely NO!

I've tried all those methods and a whole bunch more (remember the table-scrap incident!) and I've come to the conclusion that the absolute best way to chum offshore for sharks is actually the simplest way and by-golly the cleanest way too. Even though overly-aggressive shark anglers often try to force the issue with fancy chumming machines, electronic calls, and barrels of chum, all a fisherman really has to do is put the right scent under the nose of a shark. After successfully fine-tuning the their olfactory system for millions of years, Mother Nature has turned sharks into pretty efficient bloodhounds, give 'em a little whiff of something they recognize as food and they'll find your baits.

So what we're going to do is take that 50 pounds of mackerel and run it through a grinder. We need to do this a few days before our shark trip because we'll want to freeze the chum solid before we go fishing. If we're really on top of our game, instead of putting all the chum in a single five gallon bucket we'll freeze it in a few one or two gallon containers or bags.

How much chum are we going to need? Over the years I've found that when I properly maintain the amount of flow I like to see coming from my chum bucket I'll use less than a half a gallon an hour. I know that by many folk's standards that's not much chum, but like I said, it's not about clouding the water with chum, it's about attracting sharks with scent.

Chum Bucket

To properly deploy our chum and regulate its flow we need a chum bucket, and here again, after a lot of trial and error I've found that simple is best. Mesh chum bags are simple and easy to use but as the frozen block of chum thaws they allow too much chum to escape and there's no way to slow it down. For a lot of years I used the popular milk-crate surrounded by floats with an upside-down bucket of chum with holes in the lid method. It worked, but it always seemed like a lot of stuff to store on the boat when it wasn't being used.

One day we accidentally left our milk-crate contraption at the dock. Forced to make-do with what we had, we simply tied a rope to the handle of a bucket, put our frozen block of chum inside, snapped a lid with a couple half dollar size holes in it over the top, tied the other end of the rope to a stern cleat, and dropped the bucket in the water. With just a little bit of air trapped inside, the bucket floated upside-down at about a 45-degree angle allowing the chum, as it thawed, to sink out of the hole. Simple, effective, cheap, and I still haven't found a better tool for deploying chum. After about a decade of using this system, the only alteration I've done is to replace the bucket's wire handle with a rope handle that won't tear out in rough seas. I use a lid from a five-gallon oil bucket that has a removable plastic cap and drill a single half-dollar size hole on the opposite side of the lid from the plastic cap.

I've found that the best chummer is nothing but a plastic bucket with a couple holes in the lid.

Even though this chumming arrangement pretty much works on its own, you still can't just set it and forget it. Wave action, current, how firmly the chum is frozen, the ever-changing volume of chum in the bucket, and how finely the chum has been ground are all factors that will affect the flow rate. As with all methods of chumming, anglers must constantly monitor their chumline to ensure neither too much nor too little chum is deployed at any time throughout the day.

Adjusting The Flow

It's a rare day on the sharking grounds when we're able to put our chum bucket overboard and not have to adjust it numerous times in order to maintain a proper stream of chum. Fortunately, there's an array of simple tricks and techniques sharkers can use to effectively increase or retard the flow and keep the sharks pointed toward the boat.

Too Slow

• Remove the plastic cap on the lid thus providing two holes for the chum to escape.

• Change lids with one that has three or four holes.

• Increase the amount of air inside the bucket so that it rides up higher in the water and bobs around more.

• Shorten-up on the rope so that the rocking of the boat agitates the bucket.

• Manually shake the bucket by pulling on the rope (last resort).

Too Fast

• Decrease the amount of air in the bucket so that it sits lower in the water and does not pitch around so much by wave action.

• Decrease enough air from the bucket so that it sits in the water at about a 45-degree angle. Rotate the lid so that the hole is positioned closest to the up-side of the bucket.

• Increase the length of the rope holding the bucket so that the rocking of the boat doesn't snatch on the bucket as much.

• Particularly on choppy days: Top the bucket off with water and tie it very close to the boat from a spring-line cleat so that the top of the bucket and its lid are facing up. The line should be tight enough that when the boat rocks down the bucket will go slightly underwater but not tip to the side, and then when the boat rocks up the top of the bucket will come completely out of the water. This constant "dunking" of the bucket will keep the chum inside agitated and allow some of it to wash out of the hole in the lid at a moderate pace.

Figuring that it'll result in too much mess, slop, and stinky stuff on their pristine, high-dollar boats, chumming is one aspect of our sport that's probably helped keep a lot of fishermen out of the shark fishing arena. But for the sake of keeping just a few more boats off our favorite sharking grounds, let's not tell those folks that these days, chumming doesn't have to be a messy monotonous process of ladling out a nasty stew of rotten fish heads, eyeballs, and innards.

Watch That Chumline!

Just like marlin fishermen need to constantly watch their spread of trolling baits and lures for signs of fish, problems, or whatever, sharkers also need to constantly monitor their chumlines for the same reasons. Unless someone is watching it'll be too late to react if the chum bucket comes untied and starts drifting away, a pair of "gaffer" dolphin or a big cobia shows up under the boat, the chum starts flowing too fast, or the current shifts and fouls a fishing line on the propeller.

If necessary, anglers can take turns standing watch so that if some big hunky shark shows up at the chum bucket someone is right there to immediately notify everyone to take action right away, not 15 minutes after the shark arrived, grew bored with what it encountered, and is ready to leave.

Chumming Etiquette

OK, here's the scenario; it's a nice calm Saturday in June. There's been a good mako bite so you and everyone else are sharking out in the Bonehead Canyon. You've been drifting along for about three hours when some guy in a 40' Somethingorother cruises past you, up-sea, a couple hundred yards away. You get on the radio and call him every name in the book and accuse him of cutting off your chum slick and ruining what it has taken you three hours to establish.

Did the other fisherman show proper courtesy when he ran over your chumline? No. Should he have run past you on the other

Always keep an eye on the chum line—you never know when a shark (here a great white) might slip out from under the boat!

side of your boat? Yes. Did his boat ruin your chumming efforts? No. Did you make a fool of yourself over the radio by cussing and showing that you don't know what you're talking about? Yes.

OK, lets get this straight: whether or not we know that they are chumming, proper etiquette dictates that when we troll or run past a boat that's not "making-way" through the water, we try not to come by too close and if possible we attempt to pass on their up-sea side if they're anchored or down-sea side if they're drifting. This makes sense, because even if they're not sharking, they might have divers, lines, nets, or any other any other type of gear deployed and we need to stay clear.

That being said, if we're chumming and a skipper intentionally or accidentally passes us too close and on the wrong side, is it going to ruin or "cut-off" our chumline? Absolutely not. Anyone who watches a chumline for just two minutes should realize that particles of chum are sinking from the time they leave the bucket. Sure, some sink faster than others, and if the current is strong some particles will stay close to the surface for quite some distance, but from the time it leaves the boat all chum is on an eventual crash-course for the bottom.

Of course a surface sheen may be created by fish oils, particularly if the chum was made from oily fish such as menhaden or if the crew drips menhaden oil into the water to create such an effect. While surface oils look nice and do a great job of attracting seabirds, their effectiveness on sharks is nil, and since they're directed by the wind—not the current—surface sheens aren't even a reliable indicator of which way the chumline is actually traveling. So by no means should anyone worry about a boat cutting through a surface sheen. Granted, I wouldn't want some big merchant ship drawing 30 feet of water passing 100 yards down-current, but if that occurs shame on me for setting up so close to a shipping lane. A typical sport or commercial boat passing over a chumline is not going to have any negative effect other than what might be caused by an overreaction of the crew doing the chumming. So lighten up, focus on catching a sharks and having a good time, and don't get all steamed-up about what the other guys are doing.

How Close To Another Boat?

So you're running out in the morning and your GPS indicates one mile to go to your fishing spot. But, low-and-behold, you look up ahead and see another boat drifting along almost exactly where you were hoping to shut down. A disappointment to be sure, but since he arrived first, you know that the right thing to do is to give him plenty of room so that you won't adversely effect his fishing efforts, or he, yours. Just the same, you know it's a good area for sharks and you still want to fish as close as possible to your original destination. But how close? A half-mile? A mile? Two miles?

Perhaps the best way to understand the answer is to consider the chumline and how the sharks encounter and then respond to it. Remember that depending upon the current and the speed of the boat's drift, the scent of chum will leave a boat and possibly be carried for more than a mile. Think of the chumline as a long fence running out from the boat. Sharks swimming from any direction might encounter the fence, turn, and follow it to the boat. Now let's add another boat to the scheme. It's a friend of yours who doesn't want to interrupt your chumline so he doesn't park down-current where he'd be in your chumline, or up-current where you'd be in his chumline. Instead he chooses a spot a mile away and directly cross-current from you. That's OK, right?

Wrong! Remember, since he's going to be chumming and laying out a "fence" of his own, his fence will run almost exactly parallel to yours and be about a mile away. Theoretically, he may have just eliminated half the potential sharks that might have come up your chumline, because any shark traveling from his side of your boat will encounter his chum first and follow it to his boat rather than proceeding along their normal course—which might have brought them to your chum. Quite frankly, if someone is going to set up a mile or two from me I'd prefer that they do so right in my chum so that at least I'd know that any sharks moving in from either side would have a shot at finding my chum and follow it to my boat.

So how close can someone get without competing with you chumline? There's nothing set in stone here, because so much of it depends on the dynamics of each particular area. But in open waters I'd say that the distance between boats should be a minimum of three miles. Any closer than that and you'll likely be competing for the same sharks.

Grinding Your Own Chum

I've got a decent size grinder run by a half-horsepower electric motor, which pushes chum through a four-inch grinding plate almost as fast as I can drop the fish parts into the throat of the machine. The grinder will handle whole fish up to about two pounds, after that I have to cut them into smaller pieces. When grinding frozen chunks or fish with very tough skin it'll sometimes bind up, requiring me to shut it down, take the plate and cutter out, and clear out the clog. But if I take my time and don't try to force-feed it the grinder will fill a five-

Anglers can put anything they want into their chum grinder as long as it's fish, or fish!

gallon bucket in less then 10 minutes. And for the amount of chum I go through each season, I need that kind of speed.

But before I started sharking for a living I had nothing more than an inexpensive hand grinder that would clamp to a table or bench. With only a two and three quarter inch plate, the grinder could only put out about five gallons an hour. But as I was only sharking a day or two a week, the low output wasn't much of a problem and I figured that all the cranking on the grinder was good exercise for when I'd be cranking on a fishing reel!

It sure is easy just to go out and buy chum. But anglers who make their own have an advantage in that they'll know and control exactly what goes into it the chum, how fresh it is, how finely ground

Small to medium size plates should be used on chum grinders so the chum is not so coarse that it feeds the sharks.

it is, and how they wish to package and freeze it. All these variables allow fishermen to customize their chum to meet their own specific fishing needs and avoid problems often encountered with store bought chum. For instance, I've been in tackle shops that only sell chum in five-gallon buckets. That kind of quantity is fine if all you do is fish full-day trips. But the guy who just wants to go out for a few hours in the morning is going to be stuck with spending money on chum he'll either throw out or will have to bring home, refreeze and use later—which of course won't be as good a quality the second time out. By making their own chum, anglers can freeze it up in half buckets, zip-lock bags, paper cups, or in any other fashion that suites their fishing needs and freezer space.

For my own needs I've found that my best bet is to pack the chum in one-gallon zipper-lock bags, stack four of those bags in square plastic buckets, and then freeze the chum while inside the bucket. After a couple days the frozen blocks are removed from the buckets. Because they're square the blocks stack nicely in the freezer and maximize storage space. Depending upon the length of my fishing trip (full day, half day, a few hours,) I'll take as many blocks as I think I'll use and then maybe one extra, just in case. I'll keep all the blocks in a well-insulated cooler so that they will stay frozen until each one is ready to be used. At the end of the day, any unused blocks are returned to the freezer, still in prime shape, because they were never allowed to thaw.

Having chum in small blocks also allows me to bring a little along on regular fishing trips "just in case" during the course of the day we decide to do a little chumming for sharks or any other type of fish. And again, if we don't use it – no problem, it goes back in the freezer that night.

Besides packaging, another nice aspect of making your own chum is being able to control how finely the chum is ground-up. I prefer to use a grinding plate with no more than half-inch holes. The problem with very course chum is that it will not release as much scent into the water and some sharks and certainly other fish (like bluefish) will hold way back in the chumline and eat the larger chunks rather than following the scent-trail to the boat. There's nothing wrong with using a grinder with a plate that has holes smaller than half-inch, but I certainly wouldn't want to use anything larger.

Buying Chum

Buying chum is the only option for a lot of fishermen, and there's nothing wrong with that as long as the chum they're getting is of good quality and they're able to adapt their chumming techniques to accommodate the packaging of the product.

If you're lucky enough to find a shop that makes its own chum, don't' hesitate to ask what they put into it and how finely its ground. Most shops, however, buy their chum from bait dealers who probably also get it from someone else. If it's mackerel or menhaden it will likely be marketed as such, but besides that, if it's just sold as "chum" it will probably be whatever leftover baitfish or fish scraps the bait company could come-up with at the time. Not that it might not be very good chum, it's just that you won't know what your using, how fresh it is, or how finely it was ground.

As a final word on buying chum, stay away from any of the freeze-dried or powdered chums. Over the years I've experimented with some of these products and have thus far seen zero results at attracting sharks–don't waste your money or your precious fishing time with these products!

Different Chumming Techniques

So far, all that I've described about chumming has involved the common practice of attracting sharks with ground-up fish, a method which will work for most sharks in most places. However, anglers may encounter unique areas where different techniques prove to be more effective. A good example would be the shallow flats of south Florida and throughout the Florida Keys.

Florida anglers enjoy unique opportunities to fish for blacktips, lemon, bull, nurse, blacknose, and bonnethead sharks in waters as shallow as one to four feet, and at those depths anglers will find that the simple method of hanging a fish carcass over the side of the boat will create enough of a scent trail to literally bring sharks to their transom.

In these clear waters it's common to watch even large sharks cross hundreds of yards of shallow flat while on a direct bee-line to nothing more than a 24 inch barracuda hanging off the back of a boat. The effectiveness of this simple chumming technique is testimony to the shark's amazing sense of smell, and witnessing it should serve as a wake-up call to any sharker who still subscribes to the defunct theory that "more is better" when it comes to attracting sharks.

For this type of chumming I've had good luck using nothing more than two or three carcasses from snapper, grouper, dolphin or any other "eating fish" that we caught the day before. These fish can be hung overboard in a mesh bag, wire basket or just tied together with a line or wire through their gills. I imagine most southern shark fishermen will agree, however, that there's something special about barracuda that gives this species an edge over other types of fish for drawing in sharks. Even a modest size cuda will work if anglers fillet one or two sides of the fish, leaving the fillets attached at the tail, and then hang it overboard on a line.

Although this "fish carcass" technique works amazingly well on the shallow flats, even when using carcasses from larger fish such as big tuna, wahoo, and dolphin, I've had little luck while employing it in the deeper waters offshore. I suspect that the difference lies in the fact that ground-up chum particles release a lot of their scent as they sink, thus creating that "fence" of smell covering an area from the surface to the bottom. A carcass will primarily release just scent and oils that will tend to stay at or close to the surface of the water. In shallow water that's okay because it's where the sharks are, but in the deep water a lot of sharks cruising the depths might not be aware of the surface-slick going on many fathoms above their heads.

Finally, sharkers will find that when chumming with carcasses it's critical to keep close watch around the boat to ensure that sharks (particularly those pesky nurse sharks) don't come right to the boat and steal all the chum in one or two bites. Which goes right along with what I said a while back–chum is supposed to attract sharks to your baits, NOT feed them!

CHAPTER 5

Bait

I don't know who the guy was who came up with the phrase "eating machine" and pinned it on sharks, but I can say this, he was no shark fisherman! Sharks are anything but swimming stomachs ready to ingest any chunk of meat that hits the water. Time and again sharks have proven to be cautious predators that might repeatedly inspect very fresh bait before deciding to eat it or not–and sometimes they turn their nose up at everything put out for them, and then just swim away!

Admittedly I once caught a tiger shark that had a grape juice bottle in its stomach, but that species has a reputation for ingesting some pretty off-the-wall objects. And who's to say that Mr. Tiger didn't circle and inspect that bottle for a day and a half before finally deciding to eat it? The point I'm trying to make here is that even though sharks will sometimes rush in and chomp down on the first thing that resembles a meal (or a breakfast drink) most of the time they're quite selective about what they'll eat. Consequently, anglers need to make the effort to provide their quarry with fresh, top-quality baits presented in a manner that will induce a strike by even the most finicky of sharks.

Fresh or Frozen?

Any chunk of meat in the sea could potentially become a meal for a shark, but forget the stories about fishing with baby pigs, road kills, and the neighbor's cat. When it comes to shark bait, fishermen have the option of fish or squid and that's about it. After all, do you really have time to wait for sharks to decide if the chicken leg you have on your hook is something it wants to eat? It's sometimes hard enough to get them to bite a nice fresh fish fillet, let alone a hunk of meat from a critter the shark has never seen or smelled before.

Fresh fish should be the number-one choice of every shark

fisherman, and if fresh is not available, properly frozen fish of certain species can be a good second choice. But not all fish goes through the freezing process and comes out of it fit to be considered a quality shark bait. I never freeze bluefish or menhaden, but bonito, false albacore and mackerel routinely find their way into my freezer so that they're ready to use on days when fresh bait is not available. Of course, just like fish that goes into the freezer for human consumption, anything that will be used for shark bait needs to be properly prepared, wrapped, and then not left in the freezer more than a month or so.

One for the best ways I've found to maintain freshness in frozen shark baits for long (but not indefinite) periods of time is to "glaze" the bait by quickly freezing it solid then repeatedly dipping it in very cold ice-water. Between each dipping the bait is returned to the freezer for five minutes or so to allow the new coat of ice-water to freeze solid. Similar to the way some candles are made by constantly dipping them in wax until the wax builds up to the desired thickness, six to eight dips of the bait will allow a layer of ice to build-up over exposed surfaces (even inside the mouth and exposed body cavity) effectively sealing all parts from exposure to air and the threat of becoming freezer-burned. After glazing, the baits need only be kept in plastic bags inside the freezer until it's time to take them fishing.

One barracuda can attract a lot of sharks.

Acquiring Bait

One good thing about shark fishing is that with just a little bit of effort anglers can often get away with little or no outlay of cash for bait. By keeping good relations with other fishermen, fish cleaners, marina personnel, and fish dealers, fresh baitfish and fish parts may often be free for the taking. Of course, if shark anglers want to take advantage of all the opportunities, they can't be afraid to get a little "yucky" in the process. Almost every summer evening I can be found up to my elbows in glop, digging through the marina fish-head barrels as I scrounge for the fresh heads and parts that will become tomorrow's baits. No one ever said sharking was glamorous!

When shark fishermen spread the word that they're in need of bait, fellow anglers are often happy to help out by bringing back bonito, false albacore, or other incidental catches they make while fishing for more "desirable" species. They're also usually more than happy to give away the fish heads and carcasses as they clean their daily catch. Heads, bellies, and skins, depending upon the size and the species, all can make decent shark bait as long as it's fresh.

While you can't get any fresher than baits caught on the way out to the sharking grounds, a word of caution for this approach: too many times anglers waste half their day trying to catch bait that they thought was going to be so quick and easy to get. Sharkers should never leave the dock without bringing enough decent shark bait with them that they don't have to rely on catching more while they're out there.

Bait Size

Because they ooze more scent and provide a better visual target, big baits will attract the attention of more sharks than will small baits. Heck, when you think about it, I guess something the size of a tuna head is pretty much a chum bucket all by itself! But attracting sharks is one thing, and getting them to bite is a whole other story.

Large baits might get their attention, but smaller baits will more quickly get the bites. And unless a shark is very large, a big bait is more likely to have the hooks shaken out of it by a shark intent on ripping it down to bite-size pieces. Typically, a small bait will more quickly and easily be slurped down by an average shark. Of course, calling a bait "small" is relative to the size of the shark one expects to catch. Fishing for tigers? A small bait might be an eight pound bonito. But that same bait might be considered on the large side of the spectrum for makos or hammerheads. Likewise, Atlantic mackerel fillets make nice small baits for makos, medium-size baits for threshers, and large baits for Atlantic sharpnose.

Medium baits, the size of a whole fillet from an eight to 12 pound bluefish, or a big bluefish head (or other fish-heads of similar size) are great baits but they are not usually taken without a little hesitation and at least one or two headshakes before the average shark gets it all in its mouth. To counter this some anglers will opt to double-hook medium-size baits, but for the well-being of any sharks released I don't recommend it.

Large baits like tuna heads, large whole bluefish, or any other decent size fish can, quite frankly, be a pain to fish with. However, large baits do have the aforementioned advantage of having a lot of sight and scent appeal. The head of a 40 pound tuna will still be oozing blood and other yucky stuff six hours after it goes in the water. Big baits attract sharks but as I mentioned before, all but the biggest sharks will hesitate before making a meal of such an offering. But, by putting the biggest baits on the heaviest rods when targeting very large sharks like big tigers or whites, anglers can sometimes get the right size fish to hit the right rod for a change! And that in itself is a good reason to put a big bait out on 80 to 130 class tackle. If some big monster shows up, there's a chance he'll chomp on the big bait rather than one of the smaller baits on lighter tackle. I can attest that 600 pounds (or more) of tiger shark on 50 pound tackle translates to hours and hours of tussle with a fish that you're going to let go anyway. It might be fun for a little while, but eventually everyone aboard will be wondering "what have we gotten ourselves into?"

Interestingly enough, even small sharks will sometimes be caught on monster baits. We once released a nine pound mako from a 20 pound tuna head! Small sharks (and bluefish too) will sometimes have the gumption to repeatedly hit a big bait, ripping out one mouthful at a time. Usually they end up shaking the hooks out in the process and never actually get hooked, but every once in a while they'll hit the bait just right and get a hook in the jaw for their efforts. Sharkers should routinely crank their big baits to the boat while watching to see if any smaller sharks that have been circling the bait will follow it in and possibly switch over to another bait. If it's determined that a small shark is attacking a large bait, the proper response is to slowly crank the bait closer to the boat as a smaller bait is drifted back. It's sort of a bait-and-switch deal that promotes the shark to look at the smaller bait as a bite-size piece that came off the large bait it's been attacking. The technique usually works and is a great way to get a smaller shark hooked up on the appropriate tackle.

Preparing and Hooking

Because they release more scent and can have more action in the water, cut baits usually out-perform whole dead baits. Anglers should consider the size of the hook, the type of shark tackle, fishing conditions, and even the size and type of shark when deciding on the size of the bait. For instance: Suppose you have a 10 pound

The thin, tough plate under the eye this bluefish is an ideal location for a hook.

live bluefish (or other medium-size fish) at your disposal. Would it be best to fish it whole and alive? Whole and dead? Or should you cut it up and make a few baits out of it? The right answer always depends upon the prevailing conditions at the time.

Reasons to Fish Big Whole Baits

• They hold their scent by not washing-out quickly.

• A big bait will get the attention (although not necessarily the bite) of big sharks more quickly.

• They may help curb unwanted strikes by small sharks or other fish such as bluefish.

• If you don't get a bite on them you can cut them up later for smaller baits, or bring them home to eat!

Reasons Not to Use Big Baits

• It's difficult to hook smaller sharks and other fish (like bluefish) that must bite and shake them into bite-size pieces, often dislodging the hooks in the process.

• May require a double-hook rig.

• May not get as many bites by smaller sharks and other fish.

• Sometimes small fish get so infatuated with big baits that you cannot get them to switch over to a more appropriate bait.

• Can be hard to fish, requiring big hooks, big floats, and heavy tackle.

• Big baits must be fed to sharks a long time before the hook-set–this promotes gut-hooking.

Small baits will typi-
cally be hit with less
hesitation.

A scalloped hammerhead, one of
the most finicky eaters of all the
sharks.

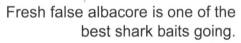

Fresh false albacore is one of the
best shark baits going.

Live Baits

Live baits can work great for sharks; the commotion they produce as they struggle on the line can be just the ticket to entice an otherwise finicky or hesitant shark to get fired-up and decide to eat. Live baits can be as large as 12 pound bluefish or as small as four inch menhaden or little pencil-eels. Depending upon the season and location, live baits may be readily available to buy or catch—or they may be totally unavailable. While buying, catching, and keeping live-bait can create major problems, there are also many occasions when sharkers can easily catch live bait out of their chum lines or off the bottom directly under their boat. Anglers should look for such opportunities and be ready and willing to capitalize on them whenever they come along.

In the Mid-Atlantic, early season anglers often have an abundance of big bluefish available to them right in their very own chum slicks. Bluefish are a primary food source for makos and are quickly devoured by most other species of sharks as well. A live bluefish

Bonito make excellent shark baits either whole or cut-up.

is, therefore, readily recognized by sharks as a meal and will easily solicit strikes. The problem is, a 12 pound bluefish kicking and
swimming about can sometimes present more headaches than most
anglers wish to deal with, by combining all of the hassles associated
with fishing with a big bait to the added problem that they often like
to swim around and tangle with other lines in the sharker's spread.

There are, however, a few tricks anglers can use to at least
soften some of the problems associated with fishing large live baits
such as big bluefish. For starters, you can use larger hooks and sew
them in place so that the kicking action of the bait or the ripping and
shaking action of the shark doesn't dislodge them. Keep a rigging
needle and cotton thread aboard for such bait rigging projects. You
can also crop the tail, by cutting most of the upper and lower lobes
away without cutting into the meat. The bait will still be able to swim
but not with the same power or speed. Using a kite works well, too.
Rarely will I use large live baits unless there's enough wind to fly a
kite that will hold such a bait up on the surface and restricted to an
area away from other baits. And remember that live baits needn't be

A false albacore head
rigged with a single circle
hook; large tuna heads can
be rigged in the same fashion.

large. Small fish such as croaker, spot, pinfish, menhaden, grunts, jacks, or most other one to two pound fish will work quite well for sharks without all the hassles associated with fishing a very large, lively bait. Finally, adding a small fish fillet to the same hook that holds the live bait can enhance its shark-attracting characteristics. This extra fillet adds scent and movement to the offering and as the live bait kicks it will sometimes break apart the fillet, increasing the chumming action.

Rigging

When putting a hook into a shark bait, anglers need to keep in mind its natural action, bait holding, and hook-setting qualities. Understandably, some folks will wonder how much "natural action" a bonito head or chunk of tuna can possibly have, and quite frankly

A typical array of albacore and bluefish baits rigged and ready to deploy. If they spin, they come back in.

I've never seen a school of fish-heads swimming about in the ocean, so I'm not able to say what their natural action is supposed to look like. I can, however, say that other than that caused by current or wave action, in most cases little or no action on the part of a cut bait will solicit more strikes from sharks than those displaying unnatural movements such as spinning or frantic jigging.

Spinning is probably the most common problem with shark baits and the number-one unnatural action that is most likely to turn a shark away. Spinning will occur when baits are rigged off their center-line or if there is something such as a fin or a gill plate protruding as the bait is pulled by a drifting boat or as the current passes over it. Spinning is most likely to occur when anglers use baits such as chunks or heads, or any bait that has more mass than length and little keel area to keep it stable. There's no one way to rig shark baits so that they don't spin, and when rigging awkward baits, anglers can

These anglers picked the right bait to fish.

only use their best judgment as to where the hook should go and then watch the bait after it's put in the water. Then, if it spins it must be brought in and re-hooked it until it's right—no one should fish a spinning bait!

Offerings must be hooked in such a way that, when taken by a shark, the bait doesn't clump up on the hook, making it difficult to get a solid set in the jaw. Much of this can be avoided by using the proper size hook for each particular bait. However, even the right size hook can malfunction if it's buried in the bait too deeply. The catch-22 is that, unless the hook is very securely embedded in the bait, the hook may sometimes tear out either from wave action or when a shark bites and then violently shakes its head.

When using baits with relatively tough skin such as tuna, bonito, bluefish, barracuda, jacks, etc., anglers can usually avoid such problems by hooking the bait through the skin. When using soft-skinned baits such as Atlantic mackerel, menhaden, butterfish, or ballyhoo it may be necessary for anglers to run the hook through the bait's eye sockets, the skull, or the tough area at the base of the tail in order for the hook to hold securely. When fishing head-baits from fish such as tuna, bluefish, or bonito, anglers should push the hook under the bony plate between the mouth and underside of the eye. This plate is very thin so it allows most of the hook to remain exposed, and it's very sturdy and not likely to tear or break on its own.

Sharkers should always have at their disposal a large closed-eye rigging needle and plenty of cotton thread to use when rigging baits that require stitching to either help hold them together or to hold the hook in place if the bait is very soft. Particularly when using relatively small hooks with large baits, sewing the hook to the bait rather than impaling the bait on the hook allows the hook to stay totally exposed while still being firmly attached.

I once had a very large smooth hammerhead show up under the boat while we were chunking for tuna. We had set the state record for that species two years before and I knew this fish was much larger—there was a lot of incentive to catch that shark! Iced down in our bait cooler was bluefish, tuna, butterfish, and false albacore, and I thought it would be a cinch to hook the critter. But I guess the shark didn't get that big by being stupid. For a half-hour we tried to get the hammerhead to take one of the many baits or bait combinations we concocted, but to no avail. The darn thing just wouldn't eat! The butterfish had been previously frozen but everything else in our bait cooler was caught the day before and had been kept well-iced. The shark's frantic actions told me that it wanted to eat, and I couldn't believe it was refusing all of our baits which, even though they weren't caught that day, were otherwise about as fresh as they could be–sushi-grade, I would say. On a hunch I cut a strip out of the belly of the only tuna we had caught that day and put it on a hook. The bait went over the side and the shark snatched it up on its first pass without even thinking about it–talk about a persnickety fish! Eating machines? I think not!

Remember, even though sharking isn't like tuna chunking, which sometimes requires invisibly thin leaders and hooks carefully hidden inside the baits, or like billfishing, where each bait must be painstakingly rigged to look and troll like a live fish, successful shark fishing still necessitates the use of fresh baits rigged and presented such that they look natural, hold together, and effectively hook any shark bold enough to take the offering.

CHAPTER 6

Locations

A captain I know was taking some clients out to do some tuna fishing. They were about 15 miles offshore when he accidentally ran over a length of floating line, which fouled in his props. From the cockpit they were able to get hold of a few feet of the line, but no matter how much he and his crew pulled from above it would not come free from his running gear, so he called for assistance and a local towing company brought him in.

Find areas where other game fish are abundant and you may have found a place for good sharking as well.

A few days later, as this captain was telling me the story, he was still grumbling about the towing expense and the lost revenues from the charter. So I asked him, "It was a flat, clam morning, the water was warm, why didn't you just hop overboard, clear the line, and carry on with your fishing trip?"

While there are many reasons why it might not have been prudent for him to go overboard that morning, I was really surprised at his answer. "Sharks. I've caught and seen too many sharks, and I'm not about to get in the water out there–for any reason!"

After all these years of so much media-hype, I guess you can't blame some folks for having a fear of sharks. However, I disagree with the notion that the few minutes he would have spent in water trying to clear the line would have put the captain in peril of being attacked by a shark. That's like someone suggesting that if you get a flat tire while driving through the Rocky Mountains you better not get out of the car to fix it because you might get eaten by a grizzly bear.

Of course, from a shark fisherman's standpoint the goal is to find out where the sharks are common, and then to go there, because despite what some folks have been led to believe dropping a bait just any old place in the ocean is not likely going to produce a shark these days. So where do you start if you're looking to catch sharks in an area you've never fished before? Just like when gathering information on any other type of fishing, if you're starting off "cold" in a new place with no guidance from friends or other connections in the area, your best start would be to talk to folks at as many tackle shops and marinas as you can, and chat with as many local fishermen and so-called experts as you can find.

Researching an Area

Because in some areas, sharks and shark fishermen are still looked at with a degree of distaste (can you believe it?) rather than going into a tackle shop and blurt out, "So, where do I have to go to catch a shark in these parts?" It might be better to start off with a good general question, such as "What's going on offshore right now?" That'll let you lead into other questions about fishing areas, concentrations of baitfish, locations, and so forth. Then, once you

Spinner sharks are abundant in Mid-Atlantic waters, but not until the area has the right water temperatures and food supply.

get a general picture of what's happening out there, if they haven't already mentioned sharks, go ahead and ask about them. At this point it couldn't hurt to ask some specific questions about species and techniques. At the very least that might help you to expose some of the guys who really don't know what they're talking about. You might also ask if there is anyone in the area that does a lot of shark fishing; it seems that most ports have at least one "crazy" guy at the end of the dock who spends more time chasing sharks than other fish. Seek him out; he might be your best source of info... if he's not too crazy.

Depending upon how popular shark fishing is in the area and who you get to talk to about it, this process will probably lead to some astonishing results. Some (honest) anglers will tell you they don't fish for sharks and really don't know where or how to catch them in the area, while others who also don't know a thing about sharks will ramble on as if they do. Then there will be those who really do know about sharks; some of whom will be very happy to share their knowledge and others will be more secretive and maybe not be willing to help you out at all.

All you can do is take it all in, review your notes, and try to make sense of it all by weeding out what doesn't sound legitimate. After that, study a chart of the area and compare where you think the sharks should be to where others said they are, and plan your fishing strategy accordingly.

Seasonal Variations

Sharks are available to recreational fishermen in every state along the U. S. East Coast and Gulf of Mexico. In the southern states sharks can be found all year, but for the rest of the coast they're primarily caught only during the warm months of the year. But even within the broad spectrum of an entire fishing season, the productivity of a precise location can vary depending on the presence or absence of baitfish, fishing pressure, salinity of the water, abundance of particular shark species, currents, tides, time of day, water temperatures, and a whole lot of other reasons that we'll probably never understand!

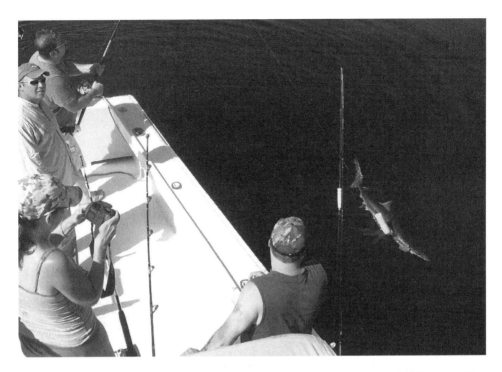

In late spring blue sharks move in from the deep waters to feed up on the continental shelf.

The bulk of our shark season in my home state of Maryland runs from late May until mid October. But we've learned that locations where we have action in June are a waste of time in August, and likewise, our late summer hotspots are typically devoid of sharks in the early season. No matter where they're fishing, shark anglers need to stay flexible and be willing to switch locations and even tactics when conditions and seasons change.

Offshore – Beyond the Shelf

Anglers will likely find that they'll be on their own if they choose to fish for sharks out in "the deep" beyond the edge of the continental shelf. Except for the waters off North Carolina and South Florida, it's a very long run to get out beyond the shelf. And during the regular season most sharks are taken up on the shelf anyway, so few fishermen figure that the added miles are worth the effort and extra fuel. That can be a good thing when it comes to not worrying about competing with other anglers for a place to fish, but it can also work against anglers trying to get a lead as to where exactly would be the best place to set up and fish.

Fortunately, anglers have other resources that will help them zero in on decent sharking spots out in the deep. Satellite water temperature charts used by those who pursue marlin, tuna, and other game fish to find Gulf Stream eddies and temperature breaks can also help clue deepwater shark fishermen in on where they might encounter good fishing for their own quarry. After all, when you're talking about depths that might fall away to over a mile or more, subtle changes in the topography of the bottom are not necessarily going to funnel or congregate sharks as well as a sharp change in water temperature or an abundance of baitfish.

Shark fishermen should also find out if there is any kind of good trolling or chunking bite occurring out in the deep for billfish or tuna, as favorable conditions for game fish such as these often makes for good sharking conditions as well.

While running the extra miles will not guarantee a lot of action, the average size shark taken out in the deep will tend to be larger than those found closer to shore and there may be some difference in the composition of species. In the Mid-Atlantic and northeast, deepwater sharkers will encounter good numbers of blue sharks and makos, and periodic hookups with large coastals such as tigers, hammerheads, duskies, sandbars and on rare occasions longfin makos and oceanic whitetips. Anglers in the southeast and Gulf won't get the blue sharks but they'll still hook big makos, tigers, hammerheads, duskies, and bulls.

Offshore – On The Shelf

As the continental shelf waters warm in the spring and early summer, they receive an influx of life that either migrates in from the Gulf Stream or up from the south. Tuna, dolphin, billfish, bluefish, mackerel, jacks, wahoo, bonito, and a whole slew of other large and small fish including sharks move in to fill the void left the previous fall and winter when dropping water temperatures shoved them off to warmer places. Attracted by a new abundance of baitfish, pelagics such as makos and blue sharks wander in from the Gulf Stream while large coastals such as sandbars, tigers, blacktips, spinners, bulls, and sand tigers work their way up the coastline. Consequently, during the warm-weather months of a typical fishing season, anglers who fish up on the continental shelf will typically catch more quantity and more variety of sharks than those who run farther offshore to fish beyond its edge.

Running from the drop-off all the way to the beach, the shelf waters in some latitudes cover more than a 100 mile wide swath of ocean, providing sharks with endless places to roam—and fishermen with a lot of water to hunt through to find them. But armed with a

Threshers can tolerate cooler water than many species and are, therefore, some of the first big sharks to arrive in mid-Atlantic waters.

good chart and some knowledge of the habits of local shark species, water temperatures, the general locations of other types of fish in the area, and any tidbits of information that can be squeezed out of local fishermen, sharkers should be able to identify areas most likely to hold concentrations of sharks.

In the Mid-Atlantic area sharks start making their way into this zone sometime in May when the water temperatures finally climb into the upper 50's (Fahrenheit). The first sharks to arrive are typically blues, threshers, makos, and sandbars (in that order) and it's certainly not by chance that their arrival coincides with the northern migration of bluefish. The opportunity to feed on the vast schools of bluefish is so attractive to sharks that even pelagic species such as makos and blue sharks are willing to leave the clear, warm waters of the Gulf Stream and wander many miles inshore to get in on the feast.

While the migrating bluefish will venture inshore to the beach and, actually, right up into many coastal rivers and bays, the pelagic sharks will only tolerate so much of a departure from their open ocean environment. No matter how much they might like to dine on bluefish, mackerel, menhaden, or any other of the early season baitfish, it's not likely that makos or blue sharks are going to follow them into nearshore waters that prove to be too cold, murky and shallow for their liking–they've got to draw the line somewhere, and along much of the East Coast that "line" might occur anywhere from 10 to 50 miles offshore along what is known as the "20-fathom line." This line is easily noted on navigation charts as it's usually indicated by a color change or an actual line drawn where the average depth is 120 feet or greater.

Off much of Virginia, Maryland, Delaware and New Jersey the 20-fathom line is a 20 to 40 mile ride out and represents a starting point for anglers hoping to encounter pelagic mako, blue, and thresher sharks in the early season, along with members of the large coastal group such as the tigers, sandbars, duskies, and hammerheads which show up later in the season when the waters warm into the mid to upper 60's. In other places along the coast the available shark species may vary, and the 20-fathom line will be farther from (or sometimes much closer to) the shoreline, but as a general rule it still holds that in most places a depth of 120 feet is a good starting location to find large, mature sharks.

If the big sharks tend to hang-out in the waters beyond 20 fathoms, where do think the little guys stay? You guessed it–in the shallower nearshore waters from the 20 fathoms right in to the beach, and sometimes even inshore locations such as coastal bays, rivers, and inlets. Many small sharks will stay in these nearshore and in-shore waters for the same reason a lot of fishermen choose to go father out–because there's big sharks out there! And big sharks don't just feed on bonito and bluefish. Given the chance, they'll snap up one of their own in a heartbeat. The little ones know this and spend much of their juvenile lives in areas away from where they might encounter mom, dad, or any other sharks from their generation. Of course, these "small" sharks I'm referring to aren't necessarily little 18 inch dogfish; depending upon the species, a lot of the juvenile sharks found nearshore still average three to six feet in total length.
Whether planning to fish the offshore waters beyond the 20-fathom line or the nearshore waters inside of it, as a rule of thumb, anglers should take a hard look at places that have any kind of bottom con-tour or relief. Hills, valleys, slopes, wrecks, reefs, drop-offs, trenches, canyons, shoals, even jetties and piers can create the right environ-ment to attract or hold sharks.

Particularly when considering such "hard" anomalies as wrecks or reefs, anglers should expect that sharks are attracted to the vicinity as a result of the food-chain principle that assumes little fish are attracted to the structure for safety from the larger fish that in turn attract even larger fish and so-on until you get to the apex preda-tors–our friends the sharks.

Bait can also draw sharks to slopes, valleys, trenches (slews), and drop-offs, but these underwater features may also be used by sharks as reference points or travel routs as they navigate through their environment. Since traveling sharks that use such contours for orientation purposes are going to be on the move, it would make sense that anglers fishing such areas would usually do best to drop anchor and wait for the sharks to come to them, rather than to drift across the contour and hope that a shark just happens to be coming down the line at the same time. Think about it: if you want to see a moving car, do you cross the highway and keep walking, or stand on the shoulder and wait for one to come along?

When studying charts for a place to fish for sharks, anglers should pay particular attention to areas where there are abrupt changes in depth. Often mature sharks that might prefer to spend much if not most of their time in deep water will move into shallower areas to take advantage of good feeding opportunities. Typically, large fish that prefer the sanctuary of deep water will be more inclined to move into shallow areas that provide them with quick access to and from the depths. Therefore, anglers should look very closely at shallow areas known to hold good numbers of baitfish that are also adjacent to deep water.

Of course, what's considered "deep" versus what would be called "shallow" is all relative to the area you're talking about. In the backwaters of the Florida Keys, bull, lemon, and blacktip sharks might hang out in the "deep" 10 to 20 foot channels until they follow the rising tide onto the shallow three foot (or less) flats to feed. Likewise, in the Northeast there are places where big makos leave mile-deep waters and cross the edge of the continental shelf to chase bonito and bluefish in a "mere" 30 fathoms of water. No matter how you measure it, a sudden depth change plus bait equals sharks!

Sharks From Shore

Anglers certainly don't need a boat to catch sharks. All along the coast there are piers, jetties, docks, and beaches where even very large sharks are regularly taken. In the same way they would if they were going to fish offshore, anglers looking to catch sharks from the shore can find out about the prospective area they wish to fish by talking to folks at local tackle shops as well as other fishermen they encounter on the beach, or pier, where they hope to fish. The Internet can be a particularly useful tool for this type of research as a lot of shore-based fishermen provide details of their fishing adventures in various on-line fishing forums. Even if they aren't talking specifically about shark fishing, sometimes reading a posting like "we were having a great time catching big bluefish and red drum from the beach until some big sharks moved in and started stealing fish right off our hooks," should be enough information to direct sharkers to productive areas.

By thoroughly studying charts of the surrounding waters, shore-based anglers will get a better understanding of what part of the beach or shoreline they should fish from to be close to any kind of drop-offs, washouts, reefs, or channels.

Particularly when using relatively large baits on heavy tackle, shore based shark fishermen use an array of techniques and gadgets to get their baits sometimes hundreds of yards offshore beyond any sandbars or reefs that run between the beach and deep water. Kites or large floats are sometimes used to pull baits out when the when the wind or current is favorable, but such conditions are anything but consistent. Committed shark fishermen have devised more reliable, although sometimes rather brazen, ways to get their baits to

Sand tigers often orient themselves around nearshore wrecks or reefs.

the sharks.

Some crafty anglers design use small radio controlled boats to pull their baits out, drop them at the desired location, and then return to shore. A less technical and more popular method often used these days is for anglers to paddle their baits out from a kayak they launch right from the shoreline. With the increased availability of relatively inexpensive, sturdy, and very stable kayaks, this method has become very popular in recent years. Using a kayak is probably also better than another alternative used by those anglers who paddle their baits out on surfboards or in some cases, swim them out. I suppose that swimming a bait out certainly adds an extra level of excitement on days when the sharking is really good!

In some areas shore-based sharkers will find that their biggest challenge is not hooking sharks as much as it is trying to find a place where they are allowed to fish. Fishing piers, for instance, will often not allow anglers to target sharks because it can disrupt other fishermen. Piers that do allow sharking sometimes restrict it to certain hours or days of the week. Some public beaches are closed to all types of fishing at certain hours. Anglers must always exercise discretion and common sense when sharking from a beach or pier because even if they're not drawing in sharks with chum, but are only hooking ones that are (effectively) already there, serious conflicts can arise if swimmers or surfers are anywhere near the area. Whether it's justified or not, such conflicts can prompt local governments to respond by closing areas, not just to sharking, but to fishing altogether.

Nurse sharks are a southern species often encountered right along the bank and in very shallow water.

CHAPTER 7

Tackle

Remember in the movie *JAWS* when Captain Quint was sitting in the fighting chair, harnessed in to a bushel basket of a reel and straining against a telephone-pole of a rod? Nothing says "shark fisherman" like a Penn 16/0 Senator reel loaded with 130-pound Dacron line on an unlimited class rod! Well, at least that's the way it was back in the old days when it seemed every wanna-be shark fisherman thought that to catch a big shark you had to have big tackle–BIG tackle.

Now we know better, because we've learned that rather than just automatically pulling out the heavy-guns, sharkers who make the effort to match the right tackle to the right shark will tame the beast more efficiently and have a lot more fun doing it. Sure, the old style Senator reels are still being used to crank sharks to the boat, but tackle has been updated and refined so much since the early years of recreational sharking that the options have become virtually endless.

Just as it would be fruitless to target 800 pound threshers on 10 pound test spinning tackle, using 130 pound conventional tackle to catch 15 pound duskies isn't going to do much for most fisherman, so anglers must consider the size and species they're likely to encounter and equip themselves appropriately. Aboard my charter boat we carry stand-up and conventional tackle in 6, 20, 30, 50 and 80 pound test, 10 and 20 pound spinning outfits, and #9 and #12 weight fly tackle. While this tackle is also used when we're targeting fish other than sharks, at one time or another, all of it has been used successfully for sharks.

Suffice it to say that the rods and reels someone might purchase these days to use as "shark tackle" are not likely going to have any unique features over what a non-shark fisherman might employ for other types of big game fishing. The same tackle someone might purchase to use for bluefish, tuna, billfish, tarpon, or even bottom fishing, will likely be quite adequate for catching sharks providing the sharks are of the appropriate size.

Just as with any other type of fishing, shark anglers should strive to purchase the best quality tackle they can afford. Sharkers need stuff that's made to endure the harsh saltwater environment, has good line capacity, and a smooth drag. Lever-drag reels aren't a prerequisite, but the ability to adjust the drag during a fight can surley be an advantage.

Heavy Tackle

Back in the early 80's there was a particular 16/0 Senator reel on a huge Fenwick rod that was sold and re-sold between members of our shark club four times within two fishing seasons. The first guy bought the outfit new, used it a couple times and realized it was way too much rod for his 22 foot boat. He sold it to another fellow who caught one shark on it and decided it was unsafe to use standing up, claiming that he felt as though he was going to be pulled overboard by it. So he sold the outfit to another club member who found that it wouldn't fit in the rod locker on his boat. I think the fourth fellow just bought it to hang on his rec-room wall–it's probably still there.

If the goal is to have fun while catching sharks, you've gotta know that heavy tackle of 80 to 130 class is going to kill a lot of the enjoyment of battling fish under 300 pounds. The term "heavy tackle" doesn't just apply to the breaking strength of the line, it also does a good job of describing the physical weight of the rod and reel–heavy! Even without a fish pulling on the other end, it's no treat to hold on to this tackle and try to move about a boat, particularly when choppy seas or a cluttered deck are involved. Add the constant tug of a fish and anglers may find that a lot of the "fun factor" of their battle is lost just dealing with the cumbersome equipment.

But then again, on any given trip no one knows what Mother Nature might send their way. So even though we rarely fish with our heavy tackle, I still like to keep at least one or two "elephant guns" aboard just in case some big monster slides its way up my chum-line. Before acquiring such extreme tackle, anglers need to make a realistic assessment of whether or not they can both practically and safely use it. Heavy tackle is simply not suited for some fishermen or some boats. Even when fighting a modest size fish, if something goes wrong someone can get seriously hurt, very quickly. In most cases this equipment should not be used by children or anglers of small stature because an inherent danger of using this tackle is the heavy drag settings that often accompany it. Drag settings of 20 to 50 pounds might not sound like a lot, but if you've ever tried holding a bent rod with that much force applied to the tip, then you know how much force that really is—and that force is trying to pull you over-board!

The high breaking strength of the line doesn't help to make things any safer for the angler. While fighting a large fish (it doesn't even have to be a shark) if somehow the line gets wrapped around the rod tip, or the reel locks up, the angler will effectively be holding against 80 to 130 pounds of drag! If that same angler is harnessed-in to the reel (which is usually the case with heavy tackle) whether they're sitting in a chair or standing up there's a risk of being pulled overboard–it's happened many times. There's nothing wrong with us-ing heavy tackle, but anglers must take extra caution and be aware of these inherent dangers.

Besides the physical capabilities of the angler, the practical-ity of using heavy tackle can also be dictated by the boat. While it's usually no problem aboard an average sportfishing vessel with a large cockpit and a sturdy fighting chair, the typical 20-something center console that might feature low gunwales, little deck space, and no fighting chair, can present fishermen with difficulties using conventional heavy tackle. With such boats being better suited to stand-up fishing, rods designed for such use are usually the best option. Such rods are usually short and have a very fast taper that al-lows for a flexible tip section while maintaining plenty of lifting power in the lower half. These rods are also available with bent-butts that provide even greater leverage for the stand-up angler. Unfortunately, because they don't fit as easily in rod holders or racks, rods with curved butts can create a stowage problem on some small boats.

Medium Tackle

Medium tackle of the 30 to 50 pound class will typically prove to be the best all-around choice for anglers dealing with sharks in the 50 to 300 pound range. This tackle should allow fishermen the chance to enjoy a "sporty" enough fight with the smaller sharks while still providing adequate backbone and line capacity to have a reasonable chance of landing most of the larger sharks they might encounter. Here again, quality tackle with smooth drags are essential, lever drags help, and stand-up or conventional trolling type rods can be used depending upon the configuration of the boat and the preferences of the angler.

Even with medium tackle it always helps to have a mate standing by to help keep the angler and the rod where they belong—in the boat!

A nice thing about using this size tackle is that there are a number of manufacturers that put out affordable 30 to 50 pound class reels that are relatively compact, lightweight, feature one-piece frames and high-tech sealed drags, have plenty of line capacity, and are tough enough to stand up to years of abuse by both fish and fisherman. There are also rods that weigh mere ounces but have the strength and backbone to put a hurting on big fish without killing the fisherman in the process.

There's a lot of great equipment on the market these days, but having so much to choose from can sometimes make it more difficult to zero in on what to buy. So much depends upon the individual angler's needs (and wallet) but as a general rule I can say that fishermen should start by steering away from any of the low-end "best value" rods or reels. If the competitors are selling similar tackle at $250, but one company has a rod or reel at $115, there's a reason it's so cheap–and that "reason" is going to show itself either in the middle of a battle with a big fish or a year after buying the tackle when it starts to self-destruct. With normal use and care quality tackle will last for decades, and always get the job done when it's needed the most.

Shark fishermen should also know that they don't need reels with a lot of extra features. In my book to much "stuff" on a reel just means more weight, expense, and maintenance. Anglers should look for heavy and medium tackle reels that hold 500 or more yards of line, and feature one-piece frames and smooth lever drags. The only reason I can see to spend the extra money for models with two-speeds, ergonomic handles, fancy colors, and extra-wide spools, is if anglers need those features for other types of fishing—because they're not needed to for sharking.

Light Tackle

In this game, what's considered to be "light tackle" is all relative to the size of the shark at the end of the line. When a fisherman whips up on a 12 pound sharpnose on 50 pound tackle he'll likely figure he's using more of a winch than a rod. Later that day that same angler will be whistling a different tune when he finds himself connected to a 2000 pound great white on the same tackle. Whether or not a shark fisherman particularly wants to fish light tackle, he may not have much say in the matter when his equipment is suddenly transformed from "heavy" to "light" in just one bite!

Anglers targeting sharks under 100 pounds will often scale their tackle down to 20 pound class (or less) and effectively move into the category of "light tackle" fishing. This immediately opens a lot of opportunities, for while medium and heavy tackle pretty much restrict anglers to using conventional reels with only a few variations in rod design and function, the use of lighter lines allows fishermen to use not only conventional, but also bait casting, spinning, and even fly tackle in virtually endless configurations of rods, reels, and line weights.

Sharks have a few qualities that make them ideal candidates for light tackle enthusiasts, not the least of which is the fact that they come in sizes that range from two pounds to over a ton. And

It may take a while longer on light tackle, but that's what sport fishing is all about!

since sharks often aggregate by similar size and species, anglers are sometimes able to pinpoint areas or seasons when certain size sharks might be found and then successfully targeted with whatever tackle they feel is appropriate.

Over deep water, light tackle anglers can find themselves in big trouble if what they have at the end of their line decides to take the fight to the bottom, and it's not just because they might not have enough "string" on their reels to make it all the way down. Once a fish goes deep, the water pressure and the fish's physical weight will work against the angler above, who is struggling to pump it up from the bottom. Fortunately, another trait that makes sharks so good for light tackle is that many species can frequently be found in waters of less than six feet deep, providing the opportunity for fishermen to motor ahead and stay close enough to their fish to keep from being spooled—or from suffering the agony of trying to work a huge fish up from a great depth.

Because a key to light tackle fishing is putting the right tackle to the right fish, anglers will always have an advantage when they can see their quarry before they put a hook in front of it. Whether it's because they show themselves by swimming up to the boat after being attracted to the chum or that they can be seen cruising in clear shallow water, sharks can provide anglers excellent opportunities to see their quarry before the hook-up and then deploy whatever tackle they figure is appropriate.

Sharks weighing many hundreds of pounds are routinely taken on lines that test at 20 pounds or less, but anglers must know that such landings are not accomplished with rods and reels designed to be used for smaller fish. A spinning or bait casting reel designed for 20 pound line might be quite adequate for dealing with fish up to 100 or even 200 pounds, but when you start getting involved with truly BIG fish on light line, those reels are not likely to have the line capacity or the proper drags needed to withstand fast runs of 300 yards or more. And, the rods which were probably designed more for casting than fighting will not likely have the backbone needed to apply maximum pressure.

To land really big fish on light tackle requires the use of rods and reels designed expressly for that purpose, and that pretty much means falling back to conventional lever drag reels that hold at least 600 yards of line mounted on rods that have enough grunt to let a monster shark know he's being pulled on. Such light tackle pursuit is not for the casual fisherman because it requires skill, preparation, a coordinated effort between angler, captain and crew, and a serious commitment by all aboard to stay the course even when it means that they will dramatically decrease their chances of landing trophy-size sharks.

Fly Tackle

Some of the largest fish ever landed on fly tackle have been sharks, but here again, landing mega-size sharks on such tackle requires so much special equipment and effort that many anglers would rather not pitch a fly to such a shark. Instead, most fly anglers reserve their efforts for sharks under the 100 pound mark, which typically allows them a reasonable opportunity for success without requiring much investment in tackle and time. Much depends upon the depth of the water, the species of the sharks, and whether or not the angler will be able to keep up to the fish with their boat. But generally speaking, 8 to 10 weight fly tackle will handle most sharks under the 30 pound mark while 11 and 12 weight tackle will usually be adequate for fish up to 100 pounds. Anglers who have a notion to spar with bigger sharks (particularly in deep water) should consider investing in 14 weight tackle and a waterproof bible.

As with all tackle, fly rods and reels don't have to be the most expensive models on the rack but they shouldn't be the cheapest either. Anglers should invest in the best quality saltwater fly tackle they can afford and opt for large-arbor reels that allow for a minimum line and backing capacity of at least 400 yards, and a very smooth drag. Particularly with the heavier tackle, it's always a plus for fly rods to feature a second (or extended) grip for better leverage and to help cushion the hand that holds the rod during long fights.

Terminal Tackle: Hooks

If I had written this book a few years ago I would have gone

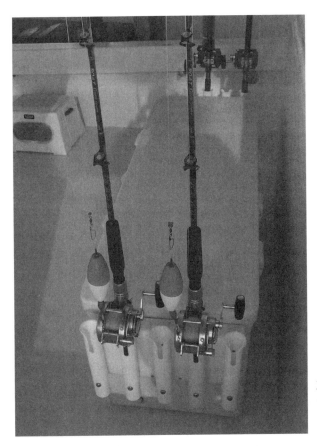

20-pound tackle with a plenty of line capacity will handle a lot of shark.

---

into great discussion about how to properly sharpen a hook. I would have explained how to give a shark an appropriate "drop-back" after it picks up a bait, and finally I would have described the right way to set a hook. But I don't see much sense in wasting ink on any of that. Because since 2005, when I finally switched to using circle-hooks for sharks, those procedures have pretty much become a thing of the past. A lot of us fishermen fell in love with circle hooks back in the 1990's when we discovered how deadly effective they were for tuna chunking. I guess because we had gotten so comfortable with the traditional J-Hooks, we didn't want to make a change and maybe start messing around with our success rate. As it was, we eventually began using circle-hooks on a trial basis while light-tackle fishing for small sharks, and one of the first things we noticed was that they certainly did affect our success rate–they improved it!

Adopting circle hooks to our offshore trips for big sharks was a little more involved because the baits we used were often so large that I was concerned they would impede the smaller hook from properly imbedding in the shark. We overcame this problem by simply using larger circle hooks, scaling down the size of our baits a bit, and sometimes getting a little creative in how we attached the hook to the bait. Even for the larger sharks the darn circle hooks have worked so well that it wasn't long before they became the only hook we used on all shark rigs.

Most anglers are aware that, since circle hooks usually imbed in the corner of a fish's jaw rather than in its throat or stomach, they are much less likely to cause life-threatening injuries to fish that are released. Since most recreationally caught sharks are released, this benefit alone makes them an idea tool for shark fishing. But sharkers will find that the benefits of using circle hooks go far beyond helping minimize post-release mortality.

The corner of a shark's mouth is thick and fleshy making it an excellent location for a hook to hold with little chance of it tearing out. Once a circle hook takes hold, fishermen are free to fight a shark with little fear that their hook might pull out during the battle or at the boat side. Also, during the fight, even a steel leader can part if it is constantly raked across the shark's teeth. With the hook in the corner of the mouth there's much less chance that the leader will contact the teeth and allow the fish a chance to bite, grind, or kink its way through it.

With conventional J-hooks we'd would usually fish with our reels in free-spool, then when a shark picked up a bait we would give it a slight drop-back, throw the reel in gear and repeatedly strike the fish to drive the hook home. Since the shark was often quite far from the boat when we'd set the hook, we found that the stretch of monofilament line was too much to consistently allow for a good hook-set. Consequently, we'd load our shark reels with Dacron or other types braided line that effectively had no stretch. The process worked, but the fact that it required extra-sharp hooks, special line, a feel for when it was the "right" time to set the hook, and the physical ability to really haul back and set a hook on heavy tackle, meant that

Eight to ten weight fly tackle will handle most small sharks like this spinner.

inexperienced anglers often had a problem properly connecting to a shark.

By the simple fact that they are designed to hang on to a fish by latching over the corner of the jaw rather than imbedding directly into something, circle hooks have pretty much eliminated all of those issues. For one thing, other than touching up the point of a hook with a file once in a while, we rarely find a need to sharpen circle hooks. We'll take new hook right from the box, smash down the barb, twist them to the leader, stick them in the bait, and we're fishing–it's that simple!

We take the barb off because we've found that the only use for barbs on a circle hook is to help keep the bait from working its way off the hook, which rarely happens. Barbs are not needed to help hold the hook in the fish during the battle, and they only make it more difficult to remove the hook when the shark has been brought to the boat. The only other modification we make to our circle hooks is that we'll bend out any offset that might have been put in during their manufacture. Offset circle hooks have a greater chance of deep-hooking a fish, which defeats much of the purpose of using the hooks in the first place. Whenever possible we purchase non-offset hooks and then don't have to worry about bending them back.

From a fishing standpoint, using circle hooks makes life much simpler. Instead of worrying about drops-back and hook-setting all we do is send our baits out to the desired distance from the boat, set the reels in strike, and when a shark takes the bait the angler needs only to pick up the rod and start cranking. As soon as the line comes tight and the shark starts pulling against the drag, the hook will slip into place.

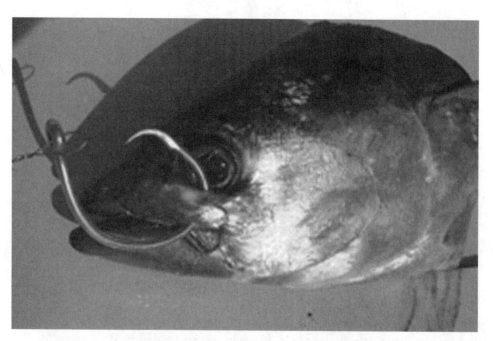

A false albacore head on a 16/0 circle hook.

Circle hooks will snag sharks in the corner of their mouth better than 90% of the time.

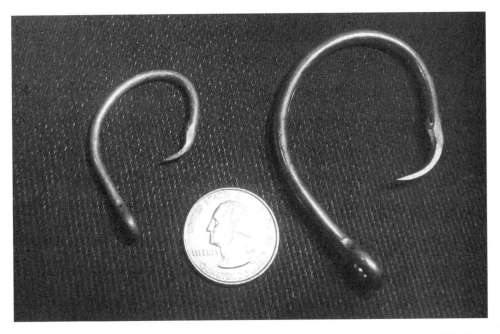

Mustad non-offset circle hooks, 12/0 or 13/0 for small sharks and a 16/0 for large sharks.

Snatching back on the rod is a hard habit for many experienced anglers to break, but the action can pull a circle hook out of a fish's mouth before it latches over the jaw. This is one of the few ways a fisherman might goof up and miss a bite.

Finally, circle hooks are so efficient at holding on to fish that even if during the battle the angler quits cranking, the shark makes a run toward the boat, or there is some other kind of mistake or malfunction that allows the shark to get a lot of slack line, there's very little chance that it will throw the hook. That feature alone makes using circle hooks for sharks a no-brainer.

I wish I could say what the best size and type of circle hook is, but at this point in time the different hook manufacturers still haven't come up with any kind of uniform sizing. For example, if the consumer buys a 13/0 hook from one manufacturer it will likely be entirely different in size and probably in shape than a 13/0 hook made by someone else. Which means that unless anglers know exactly what size and brand they want, and the particular tackle shop carries exactly what they are looking for, the best they can do is examine all the options in the store until they find a hook that looks like it's about what they need. I can say, however, that what we've been using for sharks have been non-offset 13/0 and 16/0 circle hooks made by the Mustad Company. The 13/0 hooks are used for the smaller three to five foot sharks we typically catch in the nearshore waters, while the 16/0 hooks work better when we are fishing farther offshore with larger baits for larger sharks.

Leaders

We may have made a dramatic change in the type of hooks that we use but out leaders have remained virtually the same since the 1970's. A shark leader should be a two part affair with a relatively short length of single-strand stainless wire with the hook attached at one end and a sturdy barrel swivel at the other. Then, attached at the other end of the barrel swivel, is a longer length of either heavy monofilament leader material or multi-strand stainless steel cable leader with a loop at the terminal end.

There are a number of reasons why we use this leader configuration. First, we attach single strand wire instead of cable to the hook because during a long fight some sharks can actually grind their way through cable leader a few strands at a time. But because single strand wire will slip between the teeth (like dental floss) it's very difficult for a shark to bite through. Using a standard "haywire twist" it's also very easy to attach hooks and make loops in single strand wire. Single strand wire is also relatively inexpensive compared to the price of cable leader.

Unfortunately, we can't make the entire leader out of single strand wire because it has an inclination to kink, particularly with sharks that like to roll or jump. One small kink in even very heavy wire will weaken it dramatically and most likely result in a lost fish. So the idea is to make the single strand part of the wire leader just long

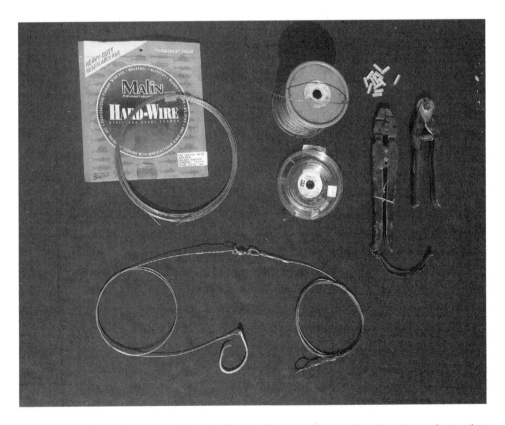

All the makings for a cable shark rig. For a mono rig simply replace the cable part of the leader with 250-400 pound mono.

enough that it will easily pass out of the mouth and clear the animal's teeth before transitioning to the main body of the leader.

The main body of the leader has a couple requirements; first it must have enough abrasion resistance that the rough skin of the shark will not chafe through it, and then it must be long enough that it will extend back beyond the tail of the shark to prevent the tail from contacting the actual fishing line. To accomplish this, the leader's main body will be made of either cable or heavy monofilament. Because the monofilament is cheaper, easier to work with, and the larger diameter makes it a bit safer and easier on the hands, it's the material of choice for most of our shark rigs.

As a rule of thumb, anglers should always make their leaders at least 50% longer than the sharks they expect to catch. The extra length will not only keep their fishing lines back beyond the tail, it will also provide a little extra protection for the line should the shark roll up in the leader. Many tackle shops have on their shelves pre-made "shark rigs" available for sale. I would caution prospective buyers to take a very close look at the design and construction of such rigs and make sure they're made properly and with the right materials before wasting money and possibly losing a good fish on them. Many of the shark rigs produced by major tackle manufacturers are either designed wrong, sloppily made, or are absolute junk. The best rigs sold are usually made by someone who works at the shop and actually knows something about local shark fishing.

When building shark rigs for the small nearshore sharks, we'll start with a 12/0 or 13/0 circle hook and attach three feet of #9 single strand wire, then a 150 pound barrel swivel (expensive ball bearing swivels are not needed), to which we crimp or tie six feet of 150 pound monofilament leader, and then finish it by crimping or tying a simple loop at the end. While this rig is relatively light, it has enough beef to it that it should still hold up even if a larger than expected shark sneaks in and picks it up.

When targeting larger sharks in the 100 to 500 pound range we'll take a 16/0 circle hook and attach five feet of #12 wire to one end and a 350 pound barrel swivel at the other. The body of the leader will consist of eight to 10 feet of 250 to 400 pound monofilament attached to the barrel swivel by an offshore loop and a crimp, and another offshore loop and crimp will finish the other end.

For times when we expect to encounter sharks over 500 pounds, our "monster rigs" will include a 16/0 (or larger) hook attached to two six foot lengths of #12 or #15 wire that have been laid side-by-side and twisted together, a 600 pound barrel swivel, and then 12 feet of 600 pound cable leader. This is a beast of a rig that will handle just about anything that swims. But everyone aboard had better be darn careful when handling a fish on it at boat side. With a huge shark pulling from the other side, the cable could saw a man in half before he realized he was even tangled in it–anglers had better have their act together if they're going to mess with sharks that warrant a rig like this!

Skirts & Rattles

Anglers will often slip rubber skirts of various colors over their shark baits to increase the visual appeal by adding color and movement. These are usually the same skirts used to make offshore trolling lures and that fishermen slide over rigged baits when trolling for billfish or tuna. Colors such as pink, chartreuse, neon-red, and purple seem to be favorite colors of a lot of fishermen. I've used skirts quite a bit over the years and have caught my share of sharks with them. But then I've also caught enough sharks on "naked baits" to know that not having a skirt over a bait is certainly not a liability.

The same holds true for the use of small plastic rattles fishermen sometimes slip down their leader to provide noise to their baits. It's been proven that sound can attract sharks. Whether or not a periodic click-click-clicking emanating from some ball-bearings in a plastic tube would be enough to trigger an otherwise reluctant shark to take a bite is anyone's guess. Having caught sharks with and without rattles, all I can say is they don't seem to adversely affect a shark's response to a bait. So whether someone wants to add colored skirts or plastic rattles to their baits, I guess if they have the money and the inclination it may not help them as much as they hope, but it certainly can't hurt either.

Floats

In the freshwater they're called "bobbers." But, as that term usually conjuring up an image of a red and white plastic ball suspending a piece of night crawler off the bottom for a hungry sunfish or crappie, no self respecting shark fisherman would ever admit to using such a thing. I expect that's why in the saltwater we just call them "floats." Either by choice or sometimes necessity, over the years I've made shark floats from chunks of Styrofoam, zipper-lock bags, balloons, trash bags, soda bottles, milk jugs, lobster trap markers, life jackets, foam rubber drink can insulators, a beach ball, and yes, even red and white plastic bobbers. I've tried just about every commercially made float I could get my hands on, and obviously a lot

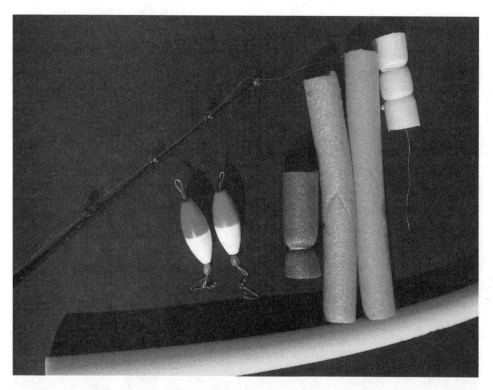

Fun-noodles can be cut to any size needed. For small sharks, orange/white in-line floats made of balsa-wood are a simple and reusable option.

of other stuff just because we needed something, it was on the boat, and it floated.

Good shark floats should meet a few prerequisites: floats should be readily available, reasonably priced, easy to stow on a boat, not have to be replaced after every hook-up, not harm the environment or marine animals, and be able to be distinguished from one another when multiple floats are deployed. Also, after hook-up a float must not in any way hamper the fighting and landing process. Finally, they must be adequate to suspend baits that could range from a tiny chunk of fish the size of a marshmallow to something as large as the head off a 60 pound tuna.

All that is a lot to ask of a float, and it should be obvious why the old plastic bobber ain't going to cut it! It's also why a lot of shark-

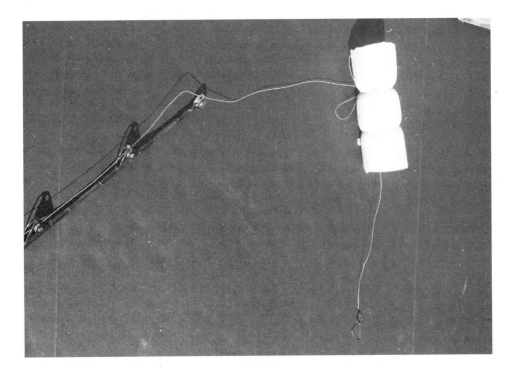

By passing the fishing line 2-3 times around the rubber band, the float will stay in place on the line. When it's pulled tight by a shark, the line will unravel from the rubber band and the float will slide freely on the line.

ers (myself included) gravitated to using balloons as floats. Cheap, easy to find, multiple colors to distinguish one bait from another, different sizes for different size baits, and on hook-up they were rigged to pop or break off and be out of the way during the fight. For a lot of years balloons were the best alternative we had for shark floats. But they weren't perfect; balloons would often not release properly from the line (particularly when taken by small sharks), the broken balloon would often stay on the line and hang up in the rod guides, and when holding up very heavy baits on choppy days balloons would often pop or break free thanks to the constant snatching by wave action. The last straw that sent a lot of us sharkers looking for alternatives to balloons was when we learned that whales, dolphins, seals, and other marine animals were dying after mistaking deflated balloons for jellyfish or other food sources and eating them. Even though the huge majority of balloons found offshore are released from the land by non-fishermen, many anglers not wishing to further contribute to the problem have wisely given up their use at sea.

After a lot of years of trial and error, shark fishermen finally stumbled upon a product to meets all the prerequisites. And some anglers might be very surprised where it was found–in beach and sundry shops and the kid's section in department stores. Hardly designed, marketed, or sold to help anglers catch big sharks, but that's exactly what the four-foot long foam "fun-noodles" that kids play with at the beach and in the pool can do. Available in two and a half inch diameters and a variety of bright colors, one of these "toys" can be cut-down to make from three to 10 individual shark floats. Most of these noodles will have a 3/4-inch hole drilled through the middle and these are the ones anglers will want to buy.

Depending upon the size of the bait, fishermen can cut the noodle to whatever length is needed to properly suspend the offering. One or two relatively thick (#64) rubber bands should be wrapped around the float about 1/3 of the way down from the top end. The fishing line should then be run through the middle of the float by dropping the snap swivel (attached to the line) though the hole in the center. When it's time to deploy the bait the leader is snapped to the line and the bait is allowed to sink to the desired depth. Once the bait is down as far as needed a short length of the fishing line above the float should be doubled over and wrapped around the rubber band two or three times to keep the float from sliding up or down the fishing line. When a shark takes the bait and the line comes tight, the rubber bands will unroll and allow the float to again slide freely up and down the line. At this point the float works as an indicator to show exactly where the line enters the water–a nice feature on long battles, particularly when the boat requires a lot of maneuvering.

After the battle, the float is still on the line and instantly ready to send back out. By purchasing fun noodles in a few different colors, anglers can better keep track of their lines by color-coding their floats whenever they are fishing more than one float-line at a time. The only drawback of this float system is that sometimes sharks or other fish (like big bluefish) will ignore the bait and actually attack the float. With the fishing line running through it this often results in a cut line and lost rig. However, this happens so infrequently that the benefits outweigh the hazards of using these floats. Oh yea, one more very good advantage of using fun noodles is their cost, at $2 to $4 for a four-foot length that can be cut into a number of floats, it's probably one of the cheapest bits of tackle shark fishermen are likely to use.

CHAPTER 8

Techniques

When I started shark fishing I was a teenage kid who knew as much about catching a shark than I did about asking a girl out for my first date. In both cases the desire was there, but where to go and what to do when I got there was a scary mystery. Fortunately I was happy to have a friend or two who would come along and assist as needed... on the fishing trips, that is.

Back then our first fishing efforts weren't exactly too technical either, with nothing more than a depth finder (that wouldn't read over 100 feet) a CB radio, and a compass, we rarely knew where we were on a chart. The best we could do is run off in a general direction, shut down, and start to fish when we thought we were even remotely close to our destination. Sometimes we didn't even worry about where we were going, we just went out on the ocean and started fishing. As one might guess our early efforts led to mixed results. A lot of skunks came home with us those days, but every now and then just by dumb-luck we'd end up in the right place and actually catch a shark or two.

These days there's no more running out and setting up just any old place, because electronics make it too easy to fish exactly where we want–just punch in the coordinates and go. Now our tactics can be catered specifically to the location we're fishing, which actually puts an additional burden on the fisherman because even though our electronics can provide us with some pretty precise information about where we're at and where we're going, they still can't tell us what to do when we get there! It's probably good that anglers still have at least a little part in the success (or failure) of a fishing trip.

Drifting

Anglers shark fishing from boats have the option to drift, anchor, or troll, with most choosing to drift. But even though drifting is the most popular method, that doesn't mean it's always the best. Drift fishing is the right method to use only when and where certain conditions warrant.

Reasons to drift:

• Sharks are known to be scattered throughout a large area.

• Anglers don't know specific areas where they might encounter sharks.

• The depth of the water is too deep to anchor.

• The wind and current are working so strongly against each other that the fishing lines of an anchored boat would drift up off the bow and risk tangling in the anchor line.

As described in the chapter on chumming, anglers who drift must choose the appropriate place to start so that their boat and chumline are carried in a direction that will allow them to take advantage of as much bottom structure as possible. Depending on their configuration, some boats will drift better with either the port or starboard side to the wind. So upon arrival at the proper starting point, captains should point their boat so that the side they wish to deploy their lines from faces the windward side.

At shut-down the captain should start by recording the vessel's precise coordinates for planning future drifts and to use in the event of any unexpected emergency situation that might require such information. Hopefully, during the last 15 minutes or so of running out, someone aboard prepared the chum bucket by loading it with chum and tying it off to the proper cleat so that the chumming can start immediately after the boat comes to a stop. Once the chum bucket is in

Glassy calm days are always more pleasant, but they may require anglers to alter their normal fishing techniques.

the water anglers can direct their efforts to their baits.

Anchoring

Years ago a well respected elderly captain, who had extensive experience at catching just about every big game offshore species except sharks, asked me: "If sharks are usually caught over bottom structure or drop-offs, instead of drifting and only being in productive water for short periods of the day, why not anchor over good bottom and catch sharks all day?"

At first I dismissed his suggestion. After all, this guy didn't even like shark fishing! But the more I thought about it, the more

Anchoring is the best method to use to fish specific areas where anglers know sharks are holding or will be passing by.

his words made sense, and a few days later I put his theory to the test by running out and anchoring up-current of one of the humps that we would usually drift across. No sooner had we started fishing than I realized an advantage to sharking on the anchor I hadn't even thought about; pointed into the choppy sea the boat sat very nicely without the customary side-to-side roll that normally goes along with drifting in the trough of the waves. Less roll meant it was easier to work on deck and less chance that any of my charter clients would get seasick–two more plusses!

The wind and tide must have been running in the same direction that day because I recall being very impressed with how nicely the baits flowed back behind the boat, almost as if we were on a slow troll. Most importantly, we caught sharks. As a matter of fact, we had such an excellent day that for the rest of that season we started anchoring every chance we got. That first time was in late July, and over the next couple months we had landed more tigers, sandbars, spinners, blacktips, duskies, and hammerheads than ever before.

When sharing this news with other shark fishermen I was surprised at the resistance so many of them had to the thought of anchoring for sharks and how often I was told that you can't catch makos while anchored because they want to see a drifting bait and you need to cover a lot of water. The next year we blew those theories out of the water when our early summer mako season of late May and June provided us with plenty of makos, many of which we caught while anchored.

That was a long time ago, but even these days I find a lot of anglers simply will not anchor for sharks. Is it laziness? Or is it that they don't know where to go to anchor? I expect that a lot of folks figure that because everyone else drifts, they should too. All I can say is that ever since those early days when we became "enlightened" we've been dropping the anchor on about 75-percent of our trips.

As beautiful as they are, glassy calm days when there's no apparent wind can be trouble for shark fishermen, particularly those who drift. On such days the boat will often drift precisely with the current while baits and chum appear to sink straight down rather than out and away from the boat. The GPS indicates that the boat is truly moving in relation to the bottom, but looking out from the boat it would seem that there is no movement at all because boat, water, baits, and chum are drifting together at the same pace. Baits won't leave the boat, chum won't leave a trail, and just for good measure the boat will periodically spin and put the fishing lines up and around the bow.

Trying to drift on calm days can be VERY frustrating! This can also be the perfect time to drop the anchor because as long as there is just a little bit of current (and there almost always is) as soon as the boat is stopped the flow of water will push past the hull carrying lines and chum away with it. Just as soon as the anchor grabs the bottom the difference can be like night and day as fishermen go from having their lines hanging straight down and their baits appearing limp and lifeless to suddenly having baits, chum, and floats being pulled easily back as if the boat was slowly moving ahead.

Reasons To Anchor

• Sharks are assumed to be holding around some type of bottom structure or anomaly.

• It's a rough day offshore and you don't want to have the boat uncomfortably rolling about the troughs of the waves.

• There is no wind and as the boat drifts with the current the baits and chum just appear to sink straight down below the boat.

• The drift is fast and will take the boat out of the sharking area too quickly.

Of course, no one wants to lose the fish of a lifetime because they can't get the boat moving before a big and very hot shark strips their reel of all its string. Fishermen should have an orange poly-ball or some other type of float rigged and ready to snap or tie to their anchor line so that it can be cast off within a minute or two of hooking a large or particularly feisty shark that requires the boat to be fired-up and maneuvered during the fight. While some may look at this as a hassle and drawback of anchoring, the advantage is that that the chum bucket can also be tied to the anchor line, so that while the anglers are off fighting their fish, the flow of chum will remain steady and uninterrupted.

The "Spread"

Once the chum is flowing it's time to deploy the baits. On a normal day we'll usually put two baits under floats, one on the bottom, one close to the boat without a weight or float, and one under a kite. Sharking isn't like trolling where having a lot of baits in the water might create the illusion of a school of fish and, therefore, more is better. Five shark baits in the water at one time is plenty, more than that isn't likely to increase the chances of hooking a shark, and it'll only be more lines to crank in or tangle when you do get a bite. The only reason I might put out more than five lines is for the opportunity to fish some kind of special bait that I'm experimenting with or when I'm targeting other fish such as tuna, cobia, bluefish, or dolphin that might be in the area. While the actual bait itself can vary, the terms we use to describe the five different rigs we deploy in a typical spread include: long-float, short-float, fly-line, deep-bait, and kite-bait.

Books and manuals on shark fishing have traditionally described the best spread for sharks as one that has the first bait out from the boat as the one that is closest to the surface of the water and then as the baits get farther away from the boat they are set progressively deeper in the water column right out to the last bait which is on or near the bottom. While this spread might look good on paper, particularly in the often-used illustrations that depict a flow of chum descending from a boat in an ever widening trail with baits set at depths that perfectly match the sink rate of the chum, in reality anglers can only guess at how deep they need to set their lines to keep them at the same level as the chum. Additionally, if the current and the wind are working at perpendicular angles, lines being pulled from a drifting boat will not necessarily be carried away from the boat in the same direction as the chum.

Under such conditions it might be impossible to have any but the closest bait to the boat actually drifting in the chumline. Is that a problem? Absolutely not! As sharks are attracted closer to a boat, they don't just stay on a course that that keeps them strictly in the chumline. Sharks will often follow a wide zigzag pattern that has them constantly in and out of the chum. So while there's nothing wrong with trying to set-up a spread that presents baits directly in the chumline, anglers needn't worry about making it a top priority. Mother Nature took care of that by giving sharks that incredible sense of smell. Let the chum bring the sharks into the general area of your baits and you can bet that they'll find them. Whether or not they'll eat them, that can be another story altogether!

Long Float Baits

As its name implies, our "long float" bait is a bait suspended under a float and is let out the farthest from the boat or about 50 to 75 yards. Except for our kite baits, the long float bait is also the highest in the water column because we suspend the bait only one or two feet from the float. If you're thinking that would put the float right on the leader, that's correct, the float is slipped right down the leader almost to the bait before it is secured to the leader with a rubber band.

The long float bait gets a lot of response from sharks because it plays upon their habits and addresses some of their fears. For a lot of years it was a mystery to me why we'd so often see sharks that would tease us by checking out all the baits without hitting any, then they'd swim to the surface and bite one of our floats. It didn't make sense that the sharks would prefer to bite a hunk of foam over a fresh slab of fish, but the event occurred frequently enough that it was obvious that there was more to it than just us occasionally encountering sharks with whacko taste buds.

After many occasions of witnessing individual sharks turning down rigged baits, but showing no hesitation to snap up "unhooked" baits we periodically tossed overboard, it was easy to conclude that some sharks are leery enough of the line and leader that they are hesitant to feed on the bait connected to it. So why would a shark with such misgivings bite a float that also has line and leader attached? I believe this response is at least in part a result of the shark's natural curiosity. Traditional baits five or more feet below the surface can be thoroughly examined above, below, and on all sides by sharks. After they get done seeing, smelling, and using their electro-sensors to feel the minute electrical current produced by the bait, they probably have a pretty good idea what's going on with it. But something up on the surface that might be producing a slight trace of smell from the chum or the fisherman's hands, has a little bit of movement (from the bait and boat pulling on it), and that cannot be seen and investigated from all sides, might be enough of an intriguing mystery that if nothing else, in order to help satisfy it's curiosity about the object, the shark is prompted to go ahead and take a bite out of it.

Taking all that into consideration, by moving the bait very close to the float, we have an offering that becomes more intriguing to the shark (because it's at the surface) and yet one that, unless the shark takes a bite, it is not able to completely figure out because it cannot fully analyze the offering using all of its other senses. Ironically, what I'm suggesting is that some sharks might be inclined to hit these baits more-so because they don't know what they are, rather than because they do. Since the bait is at the surface and the shark cannot analyze it as it usually would, its curiosity eventually overrides its caution and it takes an "exploratory" bite to better understand what the bait is all about. Hopefully for the fisherman, the shark likes what it tastes and gets hooked in the process.

As crazy at it might seem, there are times when sharks will still try to bite the float even though there's a nice tasty bait hanging just a foot or two away. Anglers alert to it should slowly crank that line towards the boat. The shark will likely follow, but now the bait will be in its face as it approaches the float. Trust me—at this point, unless the bait has been soaked in shark repellant, the shark will choose the bait over the float.

The long float bait can be anything the angler deems appropriate for whatever species might be encountered. A lot of times I'll put the biggest bait on the heaviest rod out as the long-float, figuring it will be the first bait most sharks will encounter as they approach the boat. If some big monster comes in all fired-up and ready to eat the first thing it sees, I don't want it snapping up some little snack I'm fishing on light tackle. Likewise, if a little guy shows up I'll hope that, before it trying to eat the large bait, it will hesitate long enough to find one of the smaller offerings I'll probably have out on more appropriate tackle.

Short Float Bait

The name "short float" has nothing to do with the size of the float or the bait, it's all about the distance the float is set out from the boat. I guess a better name would be "close float" but we've been using the term for too long and at this point I don't want to go breaking with tradition–so please just bear with me on this one.

The short float bait is typically sent out 20 to 30 yards form the boat, and the bait is rigged such that it's suspended 15 to 30 feet below the float. At this depth the bait will likely be somewhere in the bottom half of the fan of chum that departs from the boat. Unlike the long float bait, there's really not a lot of thought or theory involved in this bait, it's just a bait fluttering in the chum that all but the most cautious of sharks should find tempting enough to bite. Because of its

depth, anglers will seldom have the opportunity to see sharks before they bite this bait.

Flyline Bait

While working their way up a chumline sharks will sometimes bypass the deep and float baits and then swim right up to the boat. This might be because they are hesitant to eat those baits, or because they are so interested in the investigating the source of the chum (the chum bucket) that they're willing to swim past an easy meal to locate it. Such situations typically have anglers frantically cranking their float baits closer to the boat to entice a shark that is suddenly seen swimming under or sometimes actually biting at the chum bucket. Unfortunately, because of the way they're rigged and because the bait itself might be too large for a shark that's initially more inquisitive than hungry, float baits are not well suited for quickly

Flyline baits are for sharks that bypass all others and come right to the boat–they should be simple and small.

hooking sharks right at the boat. What's needed is something small and simple.

Nothing more than a small bait on a hook let out 10 to 20 feet from the boat, the flyline is as simple and straightforward as a bait can be. When we're targeting the larger sharks offshore the flyline bait is usually a mackerel fillet or 12 inch strip of bluefish. The bait will be less than half that size when we're closer in and anticipating smaller sharks. This bait should be positioned directly behind the chum bucket and fished close enough to the boat that it can be seen from the cockpit.

The flyline bait can be thought of as the equivalent of a "pitch-bait" used by those who troll for billfish because it can be easily moved about the spread and presented to specific fish. The size and position of this bait makes it ideal for hooking any shark that swims inside the rest of the baits because with just a few cranks of the reel, anglers can quickly bring a flyline bait right up to a shark that's nosing the chum bucket or it can be dropped back to sharks that are seen swimming in and out of the chumline but are reluctant to take the other baits.

Deep Baits

Recreational shark fishermen often make the mistake of thinking that they don't need to fish deep baits because the species they're targeting are "surface sharks" and will never be hooked close to the bottom. Oh how wrong they are! I don't care if someone is targeting tigers, hammerheads, threshers, spinners, bulls, or even the high-flying mako, if they don't have a line down deep, they're definitely limiting their chances for success. Unless we're fishing the super-deep water beyond the edge of the continental shelf, we always fish a spread of lines that covers the water column from the surface all the way to the bottom. Some days all of our bites will be on the surface, some days all will be deep, usually it's a mix of both. The moral is: don't neglect the deep lines!

Particularly in deep water, getting a shark bait close to the bottom is not as simple as letting out a lot of line. Without using some sort of weight, the effects of current or the drift of the boat will keep most baits from reaching the desired depth. But when anglers attempt to sink large, bulky baits rigged on long shark leaders, there's a great risk of the bait, line, and leader becoming twisted and tangled. This mess will often occur because as the rig descends the sinker will go first and pull the bait, leader and line behind it in a spiraling motion all the way down. Unfortunately, fishermen won't know there's a problem with their deep bait until they either crank it in to check it, or until a shark takes the bait and the line breaks just as soon as it comes tight because it's cut by the wire leader it's entangled with. Fortunately, there are a few techniques available that can be used to avoid such problems.

• Weight at the Bait: One way to prevent the tangling problem is to attach the weight very close to the bait so that all the terminal tackle pulls down in a straight line. This can be done by adding egg sinkers to the leader directly above the hook. This technique is effective, however, the weights mounted in this fashion can increase the chances of the single-strand part of the leader kinking and breaking during a long fight. Also, with the weights so close to the bait, any shark that decides to eat the bait would have to swallow the weights along with it. This could prevent some of the more finicky sharks from taking the bait at all.

• Breakaway Weight Below the Bait: Another way to get a deep bait to descend in a straight line is to tie one end of a four-foot length of light cotton string (kite string) to the weight and the other end to the bend of the hook, or in some cases, to the bait itself. Here again, the weight pulls the rig down in a nice straight line, but this time, when the shark bites, the string is easily cut and the weight falls free and out of the way with no chance of it creating trouble later on during the fight. This is a very effective method of adding weight to a shark bait as long as you don't mind losing the weight every time you get a bite.

• Rubber Band Weight: Anglers can also avoid tangled deep baits by attaching the weight directly to the fishing line far above the leader and bait. This is accomplished by letting the bait out 20 to 50 feet from the boat and then attaching a sinker to the line with a rubber band. When this rig is allowed to descend it will fall in the shape of a very large "V" with the sinker being at the bottom of the letter and one branch of it pointing up to the bait. Because the leader and bait are separated by so much line, even if the weight twists upon decent, only the line will twist and it will easily untwist when the line stops going down or when a shark pulls on the other end. During the fight the weight will stay on the line, which doesn't really create any problems other than the need to carefully cut or break the rubber band once the sinker is cranked to the rod tip.

• Weight/Float Combo: If a weighted bait is sent out from an anchored boat, the current will not carry it far before the bait finds the

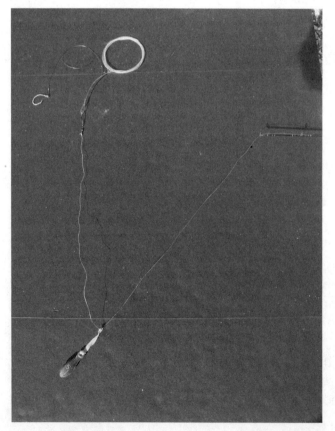

The rubber band weight should be positioned 20 to 50 feet from the snap swivel at the end of the line.

bottom and stops. In shallow water this might not be a problem, but most times if anglers wish to have their deep baits anywhere near the descending chumline they need to get the baits farther from the boat. This is best accomplished by running the line through a sliding foam float, sending the bait down to the desired depth, fastening the line to the float (see chapter 7), and then allowing the current to take the float and bait the proper distance from the boat.

This bait can be set at any depth in the water column and from an anchored boat it will always drift off in the direction of the current at that depth. When setting the depth, anglers must take care not to allow the bait to actually touch the bottom otherwise it will act like an anchor for the float and not allow the rig to properly drift away from the boat. When sending out this type of rig I prefer to drop the bait to the bottom then crank it up five to eight feet, and then and then fasten the line to the float.

One drawback to having a deep-bait under a float is that it will be easy to tangle with a hooked fish being played on another line. Of course, to avoid this problem anglers can retrieve the deep bait as soon as they hook up, or send the bait out beyond where they think the hooked shark might run. Also, because this deep bait will always follow the current, there will be times when the current is running forward, thus making it very difficult to fish from an anchored boat because the bait will drift up off the bow and into the anchor line.

If anglers wish to have their bait laying directly on the bottom but away from the boat they can use a variation of the weight/float combo technique that uses the float simply as a delivery tool to get the bait away from the boat and over the bottom they want to drop the bait to. To do this a sliding float is loosely attached to the fishing line just above the snap swivel in the same fashion that a normal float-bait would be rigged. The rig is then allowed to drift the desired distance from the boat. When the bait is in position the angler points the rod at the float, tightens the line by taking a few cranks on the reel, and then pops the float free from the line by snatching back hard and fast on the rod. When the line comes free of the float, the reel is thrown into free-spool and the bait is allowed to sink to the bottom. With the line simply passing through its center, the float will no longer suspend the bait, it will only act as a marker above it.

The aforementioned methods for getting baits down deep are used primarily with medium to heavy tackle of 30 pounds and up. We simplify the process dramatically whenever we're using lighter tackle from an anchored boat by using what's known as a "trolley-rig." I really like this rig because it's very simple and allows us to effectively get a bait on the bottom and in the direction of where the chum is flowing. A prerequisite for trolley-rigs is that they be fished in relatively shallow water (less than 150 feet) and from rods that can be cast; therein lies the reason we only use the technique when fishing relatively light tackle of 30 pound test or less.

The technique for setting out a trolley rig starts by snapping a pyramid or trolling sinker to the snap swivel at the end of the line and then casting it out in the direction the current is flowing from the boat. Once the sinker hits the bottom the line should be tightened up just enough so that the line is mostly straight from sinker to rod tip. The shark rig itself starts as a conventional two-part leader and

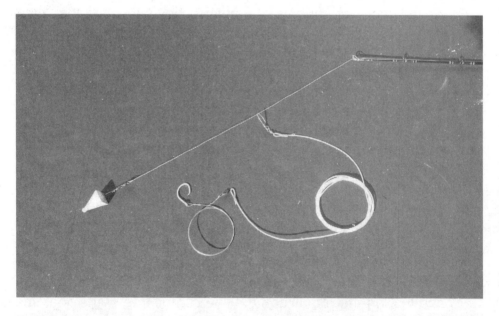

Because it must be cast out from the boat, the trolley rig is only appropriate for use with light tackle.

circle hook, but instead of a loop at the end where it would normally be attached to the line there is a snap swivel attached. It's important that this swivel be the same size as the one attached at the end of the line.

After the sinker is cast out and the line tightened up a bit, the hook is baited, the snap swivel at the end of the leader is snapped to the fishing line, and the bait is dropped in the water. The bait and leader are then allowed to freely drift down the fishing line, all the way to the sinker. Obviously, casting baits on long shark leaders is out of the question because they would likely be a tangled-up mess and totally ineffective by the time they arrive on the bottom, but this simple technique allows anglers to easily place baits on the bottom and back in the chum with little chance of tangles.

Because the bait actually lies on the bottom anglers need to check a trolley-rig more often than their other baits because it is more likely to be shredded by crabs or other bottom dwellers. Likewise, because of the likelihood of snags, trolley-rigs should not be fished in areas where there is a lot of bottom structure such as wrecks or reefs.

Because the leader freely slides up and down the line, if the shark picks up the bait and swims toward the boat it's not going to be immediately obvious to anglers that they've had a bite. Therefore, anglers fishing trolley-rigs must pay extra attention to their rod tips for any indication that something is going on down there. If they're suspicious that something might have picked up a bait, fishermen can leave the rod in the rod holder and just lightly hold the line (between rod tip and the water) in their hand to feel if anything is messing around on the other end of the line. If they do feel something, anglers should immediately pick up the rod and start cranking until they're able to bring the sinker (at the end of the line) up to the snap swivel (at the end of the leader) and effectively "come-tight" on the fish. Since trolley-rig baits effectively drift their way down the chumline and to the bottom, anglers must also be ready to crank up a lot of slack before coming tight on sharks that hit baits before they even reach the bottom, which is a very common occurrence whenever anglers have successfully chummed numerous sharks close to the boat.

Here again, it's very important that anglers are aware of the direction of the sub-surface current so that they know which way to cast their trolley-rig line. If the line is not properly cast down-current the bait will not travel down the line and to the bottom but instead ends up hanging up only part-way down, or sometimes won't drift away from the boat at all. While trolley-rigs have a few inherent quirks that must be overcome, this rig can be deadly effective and allow anglers opportunities to hook sharks they would otherwise have no idea were even in the area.

Kite Fishing

If, in the writing of this book, I were limited to only discussing one shark fishing technique, I would choose kite fishing. Having the tools and know-how to properly deploy and present a bait under a kite will enhance the opportunity for any shark fisherman to catch more fish, and I don't mean just sharks. This technique is so effective on sharks (and other game fish that might wander up a chumline) that it is absolutely a no-brainer that anyone who wants the best chance for success would use a kite. Aside from being so brash as to say "you'd have to be an idiot not to use a kite while fishing for sharks," I don't know how much more insistent I can be that the technique works. It works, it works, it works! Got it?

The reason I'm so adamant about using the technique is because after so many years of spreading the word about the amazing results I've experienced, I still know fishermen who simply won't try it. "It's too much trouble, we catch sharks without it, the equipment is too expensive," believe me, I've heard all the excuses and none of them hold up. The bottom line is, if you want to catch more fish you need to be kite fishing.

The whole premise of this technique is that the bait is presented under the kite and directly on the surface of the water with the line and leader held out of the water and, therefore, out of the line of sight of any fish below. The deadly effectiveness of kite fishing was proven and accepted decades ago by anglers targeting sailfish off the coast of south Florida. By now, live baits splashing beneath kites have accounted for so many sailfish hook-ups that the numbers probably rival the total amount of fish taken by anglers trolling.

The first time I ever kite fished I was just a kid with a friend out on the ocean hoping to catch anything we could. I had anchored my boat a hundred yards off the bow of a party boat that was bottom fishing over a wreck. They weren't catching much more than a few small black seabass and we weren't hooking a thing. A friend was a mate on the boat and just for fun I thought I'd send a whole squid over to the bigger boat via a toy kite I had aboard. I snapped my fishing line to the kite line with a wooden clothespin I had for my (bamboo) outriggers. As I let the kite and fishing line out, the squid pretty much trolled its way across the surface towards the other boat. However, the bait barely got half way before a big bluefish came up and ate it right before everyone on the party boat's eyes! I landed the fish and for about the next hour (or until we ran out of squid) we had bluefish bites every time the bait went out. Catching only small seabass, the folks on the party boat were understandably ready for better action, but even when they tried fishing whole squid under floats they couldn't buy a bite.

That should have been the start of my kite fishing career, but it wasn't until 1987 and my first year of full-time charter fishing that I tried it again. We were sharking about 25 miles out when, just for fun, I took a 150 foot length of 20 pound fishing line, tied a toy kite to one end and snap swivel to the other. I sent the kite up in the air and snapped the swivel around one of our fishing lines that had a whole mackerel as bait. The snap on the kite line slipped down the fishing line until it hit the swivel where the leader was connected. With the kite in the air all I had to do was put the reel in free-spool and allow the kite to pull the line and bait away from the boat. The kite pulled the line and leader out of the water but only had enough lift to get the bait to the surface.

I don't think that bait was out there more than an hour before it was eaten by a respectable mako. Elated by our success we quickly rebaited the rig with another mackerel and sent it back out. In no time we had another bite on the kite rig but this time it ended up being a 74 pound bluefin tuna! Before the trip was over we landed a second bluefin of about the same size and sealed my fate as an official kite fishing addict.

Since then our kites have helped us catch almost every species of shark commonly taken off our coast, and while sharking we've also hooked tuna, dolphin, jacks, bonito, king mackerel, barracuda, snapper, grouper, cobia, wahoo, false albacore, billfish, and of course bluefish. What's cool about kite fishing for sharks is that it opens the door to hook so many species of fish other than sharks that anglers would otherwise have little chance of catching.

The magic of kite fishing comes from the way the kite holds the bait right smack on the surface while keeping the line and leader out of the water. From below, all that's seen is a fish (or piece of fish) floating or struggling on the surface with no line or leader in the picture to spook or confuse a wary predator. The result is a target that's very tempting not just to sharks but to virtually any fish that will feed in the upper water column.

We've caught just about every common species of sharks on kites, including threshers.

Kite baits should be fished in addition to, not in place of, the normal shark baits set out under floats, as fly-lines, or on the bottom. Kite fishing works equally well whether from a drifting or anchored boat. However, anglers will sometimes find that when anchored, if the wind and current are both flowing in the same direction, the kite bait (or baits) will be pulled over and tangle with the lines leading to the long-float bait. If this situation occurs anglers have no other choice than to send their kite back much farther than usual and keep their long-float bait in closer than they usually would just to avoid the tangle.

Anglers who drift will quickly realize that their kite baits will be on the opposite side of the boat from their other baits and the general

Some kites come in various sizes for different wind speeds.

direction of their chum line. While some might think that the kite bait being so far away from the chum line is a liability, I promise that it's not, and remind anglers that sharks working their way along a scent trail constantly wander in and out of that trail and, therefore, have little problem finding baits outside of the main flow of chum. Trust me, if sharks are in the area they'll find your kite baits!

One, two, or even three baits can be fished under a single kite. I prefer to keep it down to one or two because we'll likely have four "regular" shark baits out on the other side of the boat and a total of six is plenty. What bait to fish under the kite should depend upon what might possibly come a' calling that day. If only sharks are expected to be in the area then anglers can use the exact same baits and terminal tackle they'd use on their regular shark rigs including live or dead whole fish, cut fish, fillets, or heads. Even though I once caught a 250 pound bluefin on a bonito fillet, if tuna, dolphin, king mackerel or any other such fish are possibilities then anglers would do well to have at least one of their kite baits be a bit more then just a slab of meat with a hook in it. When bluewater game fish move into our shark waters I always like for at least one of our kite baits to be a small to medium size whole fish such as a mackerel, small bluefish, spot, croaker, eel, grunt, jack, mullet, menhaden, or whatever is available at time. It's great when I can fish these baits while they're alive but even if they're dead I don't sweat it, because I know that the kite will give them enough action to make them look alive and fool my quarry.

Whenever we kite-fish specifically for tuna, our terminal tackle usually includes a small circle hook and a six foot length of fluorocarbon or monofilament leader. But when shark fishing and using small baits beneath a kite just in case other fish (like tuna) are around, shark anglers should still use steel leaders because no matter how small their bait is a shark could come along and eat it. I learned this lesson one summer when I took a film crew out that was making a fishing video about catch-and-release shark fishing. The day before we caught both sharks and tuna, so, even though all we needed was a single shark that day to catch and release on film for the day to be a success, I went ahead and put a small spot on a mono leader rig out as one of our kite baits. The busy action we had with sharks didn't reoccur that day and by mid-afternoon we were very concerned about being skunked when suddenly a big scalloped hammerhead popped up behind one of our kite baits. More precisely, it popped up behind the mono rig made for tuna. The big shark was so intent on eating the little spot that try as we might we couldn't get it away in time. It ate the spot and felt the tension of the line for about five-seconds before it bit through the line and took off with our only chance for filming a shark release that day.

Yea, I learned a hard lesson that day about not assuming that small baits are going to be ignored by big sharks and, therefore, the need to have every rig in the water capable of handling a decent size shark. The story is also a good example of the fondness hammerheads have for kite baits. I'm not sure why, but even though hammerheads are well suited for and often do feed close to the bottom,

---

Tuna will often hit shark baits presented under a kite.

I've come to know that these sharks, which are often reluctant to take a conventional bait, are absolutely suckers for baits fished under a kite. Weather permitting, when hammerheads are in the area you better believe there's going to be a kite flying over my boat!

Finally, one of the coolest things about fishing with a kite is the ability to watch a shark (or other type of fish) come up to the surface and take the bait. Usually sharks will make a few passes or close circles before finally committing to take the bait, other times they'll rush right in an snatch it up on their first encounter. Whatever way the bait is attacked, anglers should always take care not to be over eager to crank up on the reel and pop the fishing line free of the kite line prematurely. A shark will often grab an edge of a kite bait and pull it a short distance before releasing it. If the line is popped from the kite prematurely and then the shark lets go, the bait will sink, the line and leader will drop back in the water, and the appeal of the surface bait will be lost. The shark will probably be gone also unless the bait and kite can be retrieved and sent back out before it loses interest and leaves.

Fly-Fishing

Before I get on with my discussion about fly-fishing for sharks, let's make sure we're all on the same page and know that "fly-fishing" involves using fly tackle and artificial lures (flies) to hook and land fish. It does NOT involve using baited hooks on fly tackle, that's not fly-fishing, that's just bait fishing with fly tackle. There is a huge difference, because at times it can be an incredible challenge for an angler to tempt a shark into taking an artificial fly pattern, while just hooking one on bait and cranking it in on fly tackle is really no big deal.

Anglers who accept the challenge of taking a shark on a fly must overcome certain inherent challenges not present in conventional fishing, the biggest of which is setting themselves up so that they might have opportunities to see the sharks before they cast to them. We've surely caught sharks before by simply "blind-casting" back into the chum, but usually the angler needs (and wants) to see the shark first, so they can present the fly at just the right moment and then retrieve it at just the right speed and action to solicit a bite. Therefore, fly anglers will do best to fish in relatively clear water (the shallower the better), and need to chum the sharks to within at least 60 feet of the boat.

Anglers also need to see a shark first so that they don't go hooking something they're not equipped to deal with. One morning after spending about three hours over a shallow Florida Keys flat, casting to four to five foot blacktip and blacknose sharks that would follow but not eat my fly, I suddenly noticed the shape of a shark moving in the murky water of a channel just off one side of the boat. I cast the fly in the direction of the dark shape and let it sink a little before starting my retrieve. A huge swirl of water indicted that the shark was reacting to my cast and as I stripped the fly up into the shallower water I was surprised to see a 400 pound bull shark in hot pursuit! My fly might have broken the sound barrier as I quickly stripped it back in an attempt NOT to hook the shark. Fly anglers should see their sharks first if only to know which ones they don't want to try and catch.

The techniques for taking sharks on a flies vary from location to location and species to species, but generally the plan is to get the sharks chummed up around a drifting or anchored boat and keep putting flies in the faces of incoming sharks until one of them is finally duped into taking the hunk of feathers and hair. That's the basics, of course there's a lot more to it than that. First of all, anglers need to be good at taking rejection–they'll be getting a lot of it, mainly because a fly does virtually nothing to stimulate the sharks keen sense of smell. He'll see the fly, key in on it, follow until it's inches from his mouth, and then just turn away. This can go on with the same shark time after time, and it can be very frustrating.

Of course, what happens is the shark is drawn to the chum and stimulated to feed, it sees the fly and approaches but at the last second, just as the fly passes under its snout, the shark can no longer see the fly. It can't smell or taste the fly, and through its ampuli (electro receptors) the shark realizes that the fly does not have the electrical signature that it expected. So at the last second it refuses the fly and turns away. I've seen this same response from lemons, blacktips, spinners, duskies, sandbars, hammerheads, bonnetheads, makos, bulls, blacknose, and blue sharks–enough different species that it's obviously something they all have in common.

Patience and persistence is what fly anglers need for sharks, because if they will keep firing cast after cast to the same shark (or sharks) they might eventually get the bite they're after. I don't know what goes on inside a shark's mind that makes it finally decide to bite a fly it has refused 25 times before, but sometimes, something just seems to "click" and all of a sudden a seemingly indifferent shark attacks a fly without hesitation. Only by perseverance will the fly angler be ready to capitalize on a shark's sudden change of attitude.

Rather than casting to crossing sharks that must then turn to follow the fly, when sharks aren't overly-aggressive the best tactic is to cast in front of incoming sharks, then retrieve very slowly until the shark catches up to the fly, and then keep the fly just off the end of their nose until they either speed up and take the fly or turn away in refusal. When a shark takes a fly the angler has a split second to come tight and set the hook, because just as soon as the shark realizes that its got nothing but a few feathers and fluff in its mouth it will usually spit it out.

Fly anglers have a few options to get sharks fired-up and eager to take their flies. One is to go through their box and try a variety of fly patterns until they find one that works. Shark anglers usually prefer long and full patterns in red/yellow, red/white, or red/orange colors. I prefer something I call a "Chickenhead Rattler" that has a tail of long orange saddle hackles, a wing of red marabou, a lot of flash, and a small rattle for a little sound stimulation. But shark anglers shouldn't be afraid to try different size and color poppers, sliders, deceivers, chum flies, even Clouser minnows or eel imitations. Sometimes fly anglers will have to go through every pattern in their box until they discover what works that day.

Another way to get sharks to take a fly is to play the old bait-and-switch with them. Whenever we figure the sharks need a little "waking up" we pull out a hookless rattling popper that's about the size of a soda can, and use a big spinning rod to cast it way back in the chumline. The commotion this thing makes is impressive and so is the way sharks will often zoom in on it as it's cranked to the boat. Before lobbing the mega-popper out there we make sure our fly anglers are ready. Then, as the popper gets closer to the boat, they begin to false-cast so the fly can be dropped right behind the popper as soon as it's in range. At times the technique works beautifully, but even with half a dozen sharks chasing the popper it can sometimes be a challenge to get them to switch over to the fly. Occasionally we'll substitute a hookless fish fillet for the popper, but I often find that this gets the sharks so aggressive that they rush in faster than the teaser can be cranked away from them and they end up eating it.

When there's enough wind we use a kite to help us do the bait-and-switch by suspending a hookless bait at the water's surface within fly-casting range. Anglers must keep vigilant so that when a shark approaches a crewmember can pull on the line going to the bait and lift it out of the water just as the angler casts a fly in its place.

Of course, sharks aren't always hesitant to take a fly, sometimes they rush right in and gobble up the first clump of chicken feathers they see! The best thing fly angler can do is head out each day with a plan and commitment to take a shark on a fly and then stay the course, even if the sharks are not in a "fly friendly" mood. Anglers must not get discourage and throw a hunk of bait on a hook. Sharks of all sizes can be very challenging and rewarding targets for fly anglers of all levels of skill and experience.

Blue sharks can be quite cooperative for fly fishermen in the offshore waters of the Northeast, and in the late summer we have good success with modest size duskies and spinners in the Mid-Atlantic region. But overall I can think of no better place to fly-fish for sharks than the Florida Keys where the backcountry flats are shallow, the water is clear, and the sharks abundant. Just be careful casting to dark objects in deep channels!

My "go-to" shark pattern
is a Chickenhead Rattler.

CHAPTER 9

Fighting Sharks

We once had a thresher shark pick up a bait, rush directly to the boat, jump, and land square on the gunwale. For a split second the fish see-sawed on the side of the boat as if it was trying to decide if wanted to join us in the cockpit or flip the other way and go back into the water. Thankfully, it decided it wanted to be in water more than it wanted to wreak havoc in the back of our boat. It hit the water with a big splash, soaked us all, spit the hook, and left us stunned and wondering what the heck had just happened. If that thresher had ended up on the other side of the gunwale it would have been the quickest shark we've ever landed, but then that's not exactly a record I'm looking to set!

How you'll fight the fish depends partially upon what you plan to do if you catch it, so before they even leave the dock anglers need to have a plan for what they'll do with whatever they might catch. If that plan includes the possibility of keeping a shark, anglers must know the current state and federal shark regulations, be aware of how they will get a big shark secured and in the boat, and how they will process and store shark meat. If it's logistically impossible for vacationing anglers to bring their catch home with them then they must be realistic about their situation and consider releasing everything they catch. The decision to possibly keep a shark, or to go 100-percent catch-and-release, can dictate what kind of tackle to use (heavy or light), locations to fish, equipment to have aboard (gaffs, tail-ropes, tag sticks), the need for ice and cooler space, it can even determine when someone must return home from their vacation: "Sorry honey, we'll have to cut our trip to the beach short by a week, I caught a shark today and we've got to get the meat home and in the freezer before it spoils."

While fighting any fish, a lot can go wrong that could lead to it getting away before being successfully brought to the boat, and that's always a disappointment. But particularly while fighting a very large fish, when things go wrong they can lead to a lot more than just a frustrated angler. Broken equipment, damaged boats, injuries, and even loss of life have resulted because unexpected events occurred that boats and crewmembers were not properly prepared to handle. After the hook-up it's common for those aboard who are not fighting the fish to do nothing more but follow the angler around the boat, laughing, joking, and maybe offering some encouragement here and there. All that is well and good because the idea of any kind of fishing is to go out and enjoy the experience. But big game fishermen have to keep in mind that to the beast at the end of the line this is no joke. It's fighting for its life and will do anything it can to get free. It goes without saying that when you attach a shark that might weigh many hundreds of pounds to an angler via a big hook, super-strong leader, and heavy tackle, and then let that fish drag the fisherman around a pitching and rolling boat, if something goes wrong it can be bad–real bad.

At hook-up the entire crew needs to immediately go into "clean up mode" and prepare the boat for the fight ahead by getting everything that might trip the angler or snag a line off the gunwales and deck; if it's necessary to bring in the other lines then those rods should be stowed in the center of the boat (not on the gunwales) so the angler can move around them. Baited hooks and leaders can be unsnapped from the rods then neatly coiled up and put in the bait cooler, cutting boards, coolers, buckets, ropes, knives, and anything else that doesn't need to be on deck should be moved out of the way, while gaffs, tail ropes, tag sticks, and de-hooking tools are brought out and placed in convenient places.

This simple bit of housekeeping is critical to help ensure that the struggle goes smoothly and successfully. The cool-headed performance of a crew at this critical time is a demonstration of their experience, abilities and professionalism. Excessive shouting, cursing, and scrambling-about indicates a lack of such qualities and is a recipe for failure.

The first and foremost thing anglers need to remember when fighting a shark is not to rush the struggle or attempt to land the fish in record time. Catching sharks isn't like "meat fishing" for dolphin, mackerel, tuna, or "whatever," where the goal is sometimes to get

This mako , which took a fly, was caught thanks to good planning and specialized gear.

the fish to the boat and in the box quickly so that the lines can be sent right back out and another fish hooked up before the school moves away. The fun of going one-on-one with a shark is a part of the reason for going shark fishing in the first place, and anglers sometimes have to wait most of the day before they finally hook up to a shark, so why rush the struggle? During the heat of the battle I often remind my charter clients to relax, slow down, and savor the experience.

Don't get me wrong, I'm not suggesting that anglers purposely take such excessive amounts of time playing sharks that the animals end up being so physically drained and stressed-out that their chance for survival after release is diminished. Absolutely not–what I mean is that that tactics involving heavy drag settings and aggressive actions by captains and anglers frequently used to quickly land other types of fish are not appropriate for sharks. The physiology of sharks is so much different from other fish that whether the intent is to boat or release them, it's better for both fish and fisherman to tire them out at least a little before bringing them to boat side.

On the right tackle, with the right drag settings, sharks will seldom allow themselves to be brought to the boat until they've first been tired out by anglers. But medium to heavy tackle with tight drag settings can create a dangerous situation by the unnecessary havoc that results when a "green" shark is whisked to the boat too quickly. The best thing anglers can do to help ensure their own enjoyment of the fight and for the safety of both the crew and the shark is to fish with medium to light drag settings and allow the shark the opportunity to simmer down a bit before it's brought close to the boat.

When using 50 pound class tackle we typically set our strike drags at 10 to 12 pounds and with 80 class tackle we only go up as far 18 to 20 pounds. Of course, we always have the option of pushing the drag up the full setting and getting a little more pulling power, but that's a move we seldom make. I realize that to a lot of fishermen those settings probably sound very light, but matched up with the proper fighting tactics and techniques, light drag settings can whip most 100 to 200 pound sharks in less than an hour and larger sharks (under 500 pounds) in one to three hours. When dealing with sharks over 500 pounds it can be necessary to increase the pressure a few pounds, but this should only be done when it's obvious that the shark is quite large and not responding at all to the drag set at strike level. Even with the higher drag settings anglers should be prepared to sometimes go longer than three hours when dealing with sharks over 500 pounds.

Offshore anglers with a lot of experience fighting other types of fish often mistakenly try to use the same techniques on sharks. But here again, because sharks are so different from other fish, they react to the actions and are effected by the pressures from fishermen very differently. For example: most tuna fishermen know that a heavy drag setting which slows the forward progress of a tuna through the water, thus minimizing the flow of water over its gills and preventing the fish from getting the oxygen it needs for increased physical exertion, will quickly tap its strength and bring the fight to a timely

----

Small species like this bonnethead are fun to fight, without being too taxing.

conclusion. Tuna and most sharks are similar in that they must constantly keep swimming to maintain an adequate flow of water over their gills and to keep from sinking to the bottom. But if you were to compare the two fish to aircraft, tuna are more like stubby winged jet fighters that need to keep going at a high rate of speed to maintain the necessary lift to keep from crashing, while sharks would be more comparable to broad winged prop-planes that can function at slower speeds. Add resistance to either craft and pilots will have to throttle-up to stay aloft; since the jet needs to maintain a faster speed it'll run out of fuel first, so too with tuna.

Of course, extra pressure should still make a shark run out of fuel more quickly, shouldn't it? I guess it would if a shark would fight like a tuna and endure the total weight of the drag by immediately trying to swim at full speed straight away from the angler until it gets tired and starts its "death spiral" straight down below the boat. But sharks don't play those games. Instead, they'll employ tactics that won't allow their energy to be sapped so quickly. When a shark first feels the sting of the hook it'll usually respond with a few head shakes and then a relatively long and fast run. After that the shark will either settle down to a slow and steady pace and just keep swimming with its nose in one direction, or it will change course and start swimming around the boat with periodically changing in directions and making moderate length runs.

Bigger sharks usually use the "straight-line" tactic until they finally start to tire a bit, then they switch to the circling method of resistance. I suppose this is because they're so big that initially the pull of the line is nothing more than a minor inconvenience to their normal swimming actions and causes them no great fear or concern. Then, over time (sometimes hours) they begin to weaken enough that the drag from the reel finally starts to re-direct their course and gives them reason for alarm and a need to change strategy. Smaller sharks are probably quicker to realize that they're in trouble and, therefore, go into circling and re-direction mode much sooner.

Even if anglers were able to crank down on the drag and winch a shark to the boat in just a few short minutes, why would anyone want to? Besides the fact that they'll shorten the fun time they have fighting the fish, anglers will be faced with the task of dealing with a very upset shark beside the boat. Whether their plan is to boat or release the animal, either way crewmembers will be required to hold the leader and control the shark beside the boat until it can either be secured or turned loose. With this stage of the game typically being the most dangerous part of shark fishing, it only stands to reason that anglers should avoid intensifying the hazard by not rushing sharks that still have a full tank of fuel to the boat.

The Fight

So a shark picks up a bait and the fight is on; the first course of action should be for anglers to make a quick assessment of what they might be up against–what's the size and type of shark? Some-

Knowing that when we tagged the 400-plus pound thresher it would take off on another run and probably require another hour to bring it back to the boat for the release, the first thing we did was snap a second rod to the leader so that two anglers could work together to finish the fight. After we stuck the shark with a tag, it still took the two fishermen a half-hour to work it back to the boat for the de-hooking!

times this is answered immediately upon hook-up when a mako, or thresher comes flying out of the water, other times the shark is seen before it even takes the bait. Depending upon the configuration of the boat, the depth of the water, whether the boat is anchored or drifting, the type and weight of the tackle, the angler's capabilities, and certainly the estimated size and type of shark, anglers must quickly decide whether or not they must bring in all their other lines, start the motor and fight the shark from a moving boat, or if they can stay put and play the fish from where they're at—possibly without even bringing in the other lines.

    If the shark is of manageable size and is hooked on tackle that allows the angler to stand and fight, it will be to the crew's advantage to leave the motor off and work the fish from a "dead boat." That

A mako on the line.

way the chumline can be maintained and after the battle fishermen need only drop their lines back in the water to return to business and (hopefully) more sharks. If, on the other hand, it becomes apparent that the shark is quite large and could possibly strip the reel of all its line or be a real handful at boat-side, it'll be wise for anglers to get the engine fired up and the vessel moving as soon as possible. Medium to heavy tackle and a hot fish might also require that the angler take a seat in a fighting chair.

Fighting from a dead boat requires the angler to be ready to walk the rod around the boat anytime the fish decides to go that way, and depending upon the shark's attitude this could have the fisherman lapping the boat many times. Hopefully everyone else aboard did a good job of clearing the deck and straightening the boat up for

Anglers should never try to rush a shark to the boat.

battle, this is not a time for the angler to be tripping over bait buckets or tangled their feet in mooring lines!

I've caught sharks of all sizes from boats ranging 14 to 60 feet, and in my opinion the best rig to be in while fighting big fish is a center console outboard boat of about 25 feet in length or less. Providing there are no obstructions such as outriggers, tuna tower legs, or antennas on the gunwales to work around, a boat of this size allows the angler to quickly and easily move from bow to stern with the fish. By mounting a fighting chair near the bow, anglers using medium to heavy tackle will find that decent size sharks will actually pull this size boat in the direction they travel, thus requiring less maneuvering of the boat via the engine. If the engine needs to be fired up and the fish followed or chased to regain line, the skipper will find that it's a lot easier going forward with the angler in the bow of the boat than it is backing down with the angler in the cockpit.

Once a shark takes more than about 300 yards of line it's time for the fishermen to get after it and start regaining some line. Too much line out in the water increases the likelihood of losing the fish, as the shark could suddenly take off on a long run and spool the reel, the line could break after contacting another fish, debris in the water, or structure on the bottom, or the shark could reverse direction, put a big belly in the line and break off under the boat before the angler realizes what's happened.

Chasing down a fish from a center console boat is as easy as putting the angler up front, pointing the bow at the fish, and moving ahead at a pace that the angler can regain line without the boat running over it. On conventional boats where the angler must fight the fish from the cockpit, rather that running directly toward the shark it's better for the captain to angle towards a spot about 50 yards off to the side of the fish. By running parallel to the shark the crew can close the gap without as much chance of running over their own line if the fish makes a hard turn to the front of the boat. When they get close to the shark the boat can maintain a parallel course to the fish or be spun around and the shark kept off the transom.

As the fight progresses the angler should maintain steady pressure on the shark as the captain keeps the boat relatively close to the fish and positioned off whichever side it will be either taken or released from. When bringing large sharks to a boat it's always best to have the boat moving ahead slowly to allow for quick maneuvers, to keep a shark from getting under the boat and possibly fouling and breaking the line or leader. As a shark begins to tire and eventually gets closer to the boat it will often adopt the tactic of continually making turns either towards or away from the boat. With the vessel moving ahead the captain can easily counter these moves by turning toward or away from the fish as necessary.

Do You Need a Bigger Boat?

If I had a buck for every time one of my clients repeated the line "we're going to need a bigger boat," I'd be one rich charter captain by now! It almost never fails, as soon as the first set of eyes spots the first shark of the day, I always know that someone is going to blurt it out, which of course will trigger someone else to start humming the sound-tract music from the movie, which will then prompt the reciting of other lines, until I finally have enough of it all and blurt out something like: "Hey guys, I know your thoughts are flying off to movie-land right now, but if you look in the water you'll see what we on the boat like to call 'reality.' As you're enjoying your time in Hollywood–try not to let reality bite you in the butt!" That usually stops them, at least until the next shark comes along.

Despite the repetitive jokes about needing a bigger boat my *Fish Finder* is more than adequate in size for the fishing that we do. At 40 feet she's bigger than some and certainly smaller than others in our local charter boat fleet. But the length of a boat really has very little to do with whether or not a particular vessel will make for a good shark boat. The primary features that a shark angler should look for in a boat would include safety, seaworthiness, and fishability. Besides that, anglers need to consider the nature of the shark fishing they will be doing to decide what requirements they will have of their boat. For instance: I require a big boat for my charter business because I need to be able to safely and comfortably carry six passengers, sometimes many miles offshore under a variety of sea conditions. But before I started chartering I fished from a 19 foot center console. We were still dealing with some really big sharks, but it was only two or three of us on the boat and we had the luxury of not going out if the weather wasn't perfect.

I have an even smaller boat than that for light tackle fishing in the shallow waters of the Florida Keys. At 14 feet it's a far cry from what most would consider a "shark fishing machine" but for the (usually) small sharks that we target down there with our fly tackle the vessel is quite adequate. We can also get away with such a small boat because all the sharks we get are released. If our intention was to actually bring home any of the sharks, I don't think our little rig would be so appropriate.

Of course, as anglers use and become better accustomed to their boats they'll typically do some modifications to make them more shark fishing friendly (a rod holder here, a cutting board there,) until their rigs are tweaked out to accommodate the sizes and species of the sharks their likely to catch and their own special fishing techniques.

Hoists

While most boats designed for saltwater fishing will likely be at least adequate platforms for tangling with sharks, as soon as anglers decide to put a shark in the boat with them, they'll realize that some boats are better suited for the task than others. It's all about getting the big guy aboard. On boats with transom doors, low gunwales, or swim platforms this can be a snap, but many vessels built for the ocean have rather high freeboard, and bringing hundreds of pounds of dead weight over the side is not possible without some form of hoist.

We have pretty high sides on the *Fish Finder* and no transom door. To make up for the deficit I installed a davit on the port side which swings out over the side and allows us to use a block and tackle to hoist a large fish straight out of the water and then swing it into the boat. As high as the sides are, without this accessory it would be next to impossible to get really large sharks in the boat. Having a davit that swings out is nice, but a block and tackle can also be attached to a simple gin-pole (straight pole) or even just a sturdy leg on a tower, or reinforced section of a cabin wall.

A quality stainless steel block and tackle is always handy to have aboard. When I fished from my 19 footer we would fasten the hoist to the bow cleat and then bring the rope all the way to the transom where we would attach it to the shark's tail. The transom was low, wide, and there was room between the single outboard and the side. We would hoist a shark tail first right over the transom and keep pulling it forward until we could secure it in front of the console for the ride home.

Anglers will sometimes use cable-pullers (come-alongs) as alternatives to block and tackles for hoisting large sharks aboard. These tools have incredible pulling power, so much pull in fact that they can rip a cleat right out of a deck. They'll also rust up if they're left on the boat, so those who choose to use these devices should take extra caution with both use and storage.

A davit like this makes it a lot easier to bring a large
shark over a high gunwale.

CHAPTER 10

Landing and Releasing

An important part of dealing with any large fish is knowing when the animal is tired enough that it can be controlled at boat-side and safely landed or released. If a fish is ready to be taken, anglers shouldn't prolong a fight and risk either losing it or stressing the shark out so much that if released it might not be able to recover

It's usually best to stay in the boat while fighting a shark–but some people just won't listen when you tell them so!

from the struggle. Likewise, anglers surely don't want to rush and grab the leader at the first chance they get and possibly lose the fish or be injured from a shark that's not nearly ready to cooperate.

After the angler cranks the shark so close that the swivel reaches the rod tip and they can reel no more, it's time for the mate (or whatever you wish to call the person who is going to "wire" the fish) to reach out and very carefully grab the leader and start to pull the shark the last few feet to the boat. At the same time the mate should look closely at the shark and try to see where and how well the hook is set in the shark's mouth. If the hook is firmly embedded in the jaw then substantial pressure can be applied on the shark to hold it alongside of the boat. But if the hook is only barely holding on to a small sliver of skin, the mate must take care not to pull too hard and

Wiring a thresher at boat-side.

tear the hook free. This critical observation must be made quickly and accurately or there's a good chance the shark will be lost. A lot of big fish have been pulled off at the boat when the mate mistakenly assumes the fish is hooked well, just because it's been on the line for a long time. Crew members must remember that during a fight the angler can only apply as much pressure on the fish as the drag will allow. A hook that's just barely embedded might hold tight for a long time, but once someone grabs the leader the pressure on the hook can increase tenfold and a hooked fish can become a lost fish. I tell my mates not to apply any more pressure than the angler has been until they know for certain that the hook is where it should be.

Mates should also take extra care not to try and hold a shark by the leader if the fish isn't ready. Sometimes these animals will

Many fish are lost at the boat because anglers don't know when to grab the leader or how much pressure to apply.

allow themselves to be brought to the boat not because the angler whipped them into submission as much as they just don't really know any better–and they're still full of energy. When the leader is grabbed, if the shark resists strongly and shows little sign of submission, the mate must allow the leader to be pulled from his hands, the shark to retreat, and the angler to get back to work with rod and reel until the shark is properly tired out and can be held along the side of the boat without it being too much of an ordeal for man or beast.

Just as soon as a shark has been properly played out and brought to the boat crewmembers must work quickly to either gaff or release the fish. Particularly if the shark is large, anglers will find that it's better for both them and their catch if the boat is kept moving ahead very slowly during this process. The mate usually has better control over a shark from a moving boat and there is less chance that the fish will get under the hull and possibly foul the line or leader on the propeller or rudder.

Boating a Shark: Gaffing

The mate's first job in the process is to get a sense as to whether or not the shark is even ready for the gaff. When he grabs the leader he'll know if the shark is tired enough that it will allow him to move it about, or whether the fish is still strong enough that it is pretty much capable of doing whatever it wants. If the shark still has a full head of steam the mate might suggest that everyone takes their time and allow the fish to fight a while longer before they attempt to stick it with a gaff or even a tag.

When the shark is ready, the mate will direct the fish to within striking range of the gaff. It's crucial that he's able to release his hold at any second and allow the leader to slip from his hands should the shark muster up enough strength for another run. I'm sure I don't have to go into the gory details of what could happen if the guy holding the leader can't let go when a shark makes a final run.

I know that my instructions to gaff a shark back towards the tail contrasts with the usual policy of sticking a fish in the head or "shoulder" area. But sharks ain't like other fish; gaff a shark forward of its dorsal fin and a fisherman will lose the option of controlling the fish by pulling it backwards behind the boat, and they'll have a heck of a time getting the tail rope on the animal. Think about it, with the gaff up in the head, anglers have no option but to pull a shark to the boat pointy-end first. That's not the safest end of an upset shark to have to deal with, particularly when the next task is to secure a rope to the tail which might be a good six to ten feet at the other end of the thrashing, rolling, and snapping critter! In over 35 years of sharking I have never encountered a situation when it was better to gaff a shark anywhere but in the tail.

While I'm on the subject of what "not" to do: if you've noticed, everything I've mentioned about gaffing a shark involves the use of a flying gaff not a straight gaff. The barbed-hook, detachable head, and rope of a flying gaff allows a fish to be left in the water after it's

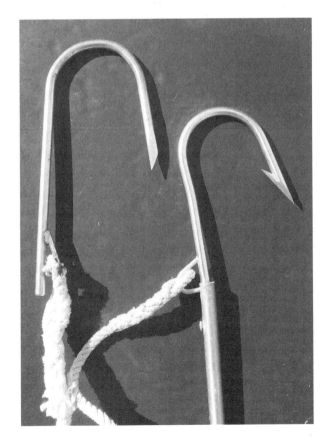

Only fly-gaff heads that have a cutting edge will adequately penetrate a shark's tough skin. Most flying gaffs have barbs, but not all; the head at the left was made by famous shark fisherman Russell Sindler and is my favorite and most effective.

been impaled. A straight gaff, on the other hand is used to stick a fish, snatch it out of the water, and swing it into the boat in one motion. Any fish that does a lot of kicking and twisting will quickly find its way off the barbless and relatively short hook on most straight gaffs, so experienced anglers won't use this tool for holding fish in the water. Instead they'll use it to get the fish out of the water as quickly as possible. And therein lays the problem of using a straight gaff for sharks–even if you have the muscles to heft a couple hundred pounds of shark over the side, would you want to? I don't think anyone would want that much live dynamite going off on their deck, it's bad enough when a 10 pound dolphin misses the fish box and goes flopping all around the cockpit—imagine what a 150 pound shark could do!

Of course that's assuming a fisherman could even get a decent size shark in the boat with a straight gaff. I know a fellow who made the mistake of sticking a 100 pound mako with a straight gaff. The fish immediately rolled away from the boat pulling the gaff from his hands, then it rolled back the other way and whacked the guy in the face with the gaff handle. In the process the gaff fell out of the fish and sank while the fish kinked the leader and got away. My buddy lost the gaff, the shark, a piece of his tooth, and a few ounces of blood all because he chose the wrong tool for the job. Unless the shark is little fellow like a sharpnose, bonnethead, or dogfish that can go from the water directly into a cooler, never use a straight gaff for sharks–period!

A flying gaff might be the only type of gaff to use on a shark, but not all flying gaffs are created equal. Many are not even adequate for use on sharks because they're designed with a conical tip (similar to a pencil) that's only sharp at the tip. Such gaffs are OK for soft skinned fish such as tuna or billfish, but to penetrate the super-tough hide of a shark, anglers need a gaff that has a long cutting edge (like a fish hook) that can be sharpened with a file.

Some of the most common flying gaffs come in four, six, and eight-inch sizes. This measurement is made from the shank of the head (the hook) to the point. A six inch head is ideal size for most sharks in the 100 to 400 pound range. An eight inch head is better for the larger sharks because it will take a bigger bite out of the fish and have less chance of tearing out. However, a larger head is difficult to plant on the smaller sharks, so anglers would be wise to have both a six and an eight inch head available for whatever comes along. It's always a good idea to have two gaff heads aboard as it allows one to be used as a quick back-up should there be a problem with the way the first one was planted.

Tail Roping

Fish are sometimes lost during a fierce boat-side struggle when gaff heads are torn out. So the next step after gaffing is to secure a tail rope on the shark, and it's not until this task is complete that the battle can be considered "over." With the flying gaff head imbedded back toward the tail and the fish being pulled backwards by the boat, securing the tail rope is a pretty simple process of slowing the boat down just enough that the shark's tail can be pulled within reach. Then a rope with an eye-splice that's been made into a noose can be slipped over the tail, tightened up, and made secure with a final half-hitch. Once the other end of the line has been tied-off to a stern or spring line cleat the shark can officially be considered caught and secured. The process is simplified if the person doing the tail-roping first puts their arm through the noose and allows it to hang from their shoulder so that when they grab the top lobe of the shark's tail the noose can slip down their arm directly over the tail.

Lassoing a Shark

All right cowboys, let's get this straight, when I use the term "lassoing" I'm not referring to what you do with horses and steers. Lassoing a shark means getting a tail rope on it by bringing the shark through the noose headfirst (front to back) rather than by tail-roping it in the (back to front) manner I previously described. Tail-roping and lassoing both result in a shark being held to the boat by a rope secured at the base of its tail, but while tail-roping is done after a shark has first been gaffed, lassoing is done instead of gaffing the shark at all and is, therefore, an alternative for anglers who need to secure a shark but do not have or do not wish to use a flying gaff.

Lassoing a shark is not as difficult or as dangerous as one might think provided the animal has been properly worn out by the angler. The process of getting a lasso on a shark takes longer, requires that the shark be very cooperative at the boat, and is certainly more involved than gaffing the fish, but when the process is complete anglers have a very secure hold on the shark that will not slip, tear, or pull off.

A lasso can be as simple as a line with a loop tied or spliced at one end, but the best ones are made by splicing a two-inch diameter metal ring to one end. When the opposite end of the line is passed through the metal ring it makes for a noose that slides closed very easily. A metal snap can also be used in place of the ring, but snaps can open up under the extreme pressure exerted by a large twisting and thrashing shark, while the metal ring is simple and foolproof.

Sharks are lassoed by putting a noose over the head of the fish, working it back, and then tightening it up around the tail–of course that's easier said than done! The process involves the coordinated efforts of the angler who must basically do nothing but stay ready with the rod in case the shark makes a last-minute surge, the mate who must hold the fish close to the boat on the leader, the captain who will keep the boat moving ahead very slowly and in a direction that keeps the shark alongside and not under the boat, and finally the "lassoer" or "cowboy" or whatever you want to call the guy tasked with manipulating the rope over the shark.

With the boat moving ahead just barely enough that the shark stays parallel to the surface of the water (not tail down) the lasso is made into about a three-foot diameter noose and then laid on the deck for the angler to step into. The noose is then worked up and over the angler, the rod, and down the leader to the shark. With the help of a boat-hook or straight gaff the noose is then very carefully worked over the shark's head and fins and back towards its tail. Just before the noose gets to the caudal fins (blades) of the tail it should be pulled closed and the tail of the shark pulled forward while the mate slacks up on the leader, which allows the shark's head to drift back. The process effectively spins the shark around, and with the other end of the lasso line tied to a stern cleat, the shark ends up being pulled backwards by the boat.

The lasso is slipped from the head back to the tail before being tightened-up.

Once they start getting pulled around by their tail, almost any shark is going to start going nuts and use any reserve strength they have in a final effort to get free. Fortunately, once the tail rope is in place the captain needs only to keep the boat moving ahead slowly to maintain control of the shark by pulling it backwards through the water. Contrary to popular misconceptions, pulling a shark backwards through the water will not kill the fish by "drowning" it, but the process will keep it under control until (over time) enough of its energy has been sapped that it can be safely pulled aboard.

The Head Rope

After a shark has been tail-roped it's usually wise to tie it off to the bow or a spring-line cleat for a while before pulling the fish aboard for the trip home. If the flying gaff head is still in place, remove it so if the shark decides to do a bit of last minute kicking about the metal head won't slam into and damage the side of the boat. If the boat is drifting the shark should be hung from the windward side and be lowered down until the base of the tail is just about a foot from the water. This will keep most of the shark in the water and the meat from spoiling in warm air temperatures. Anglers can also bleed their catch to help maintain the quality of the meat by making a deep incision on the underside of the tail just ahead of the tail rope, all the way to (but not through) the vertebrae.

Eventually it will be time to bring the shark aboard for the ride home. Obviously, depending upon the size of the shark, number of able crewmembers, configuration of the boat, and the available equipment, this task can be anywhere from very easy to next to impossible and may require that the anglers tow their catch home. Sharkers fishing from vessels equipped with transom doors, gin-poles, or davits will find the job to be a lot less back-breaking than trying to pull many hundreds of pounds of fish up over the high sides or transom of a boat. Anglers have it made if their boat is equipped with a transom-length swim platform because all they have to do is slide the shark a few inches up on the platform, tie it down, and they're ready to roll. Low transoms on some outboard boats also make it easy to load big fish, particularly if the anglers have a block-and-tackle or a

Slipping a bucket over the head of a shark before pulling it aboard can provide additional safety.

cable-puller they can secure someplace forward in the boat and then winch it in.

However it will be pulled aboard, no attempt should be made to load a shark before a head rope is properly secured to the animal. A head rope is just a noose, similar to a tail rope, that's secured around the shark at the gill area just forward of its pectoral fins. With the shark hanging from a cleat the head rope can be placed around the tail, and with the help of a boat-hook to get it past the fins, worked down the body of the shark to the head and then pulled tight. With head and tail rope secured, the shark is ready to be pulled TAIL FIRST into the boat.

Before loading the shark, crewmembers must clear away anything from the area that could be damaged if the shark whacks with its tail, bites, or slams against. A shark will not flip around the deck like

Sharks should not be brought aboard until both head and tail ropes are properly secured.

Once the shark is in the boat, both head and tail should be secured.

----

a little perch that's just been plucked from the water if it's been given enough time before loading, but by swinging its head and tail and biting anything its jaws come in contact with it can still cause problems and even injuries if not properly secured. As the shark comes over the side and into the boat the head and tail ropes should be taken to cleats and tightened up so that when the fish hits the deck it will be restrained from both ends, preventing it from having free reign of the cockpit. After it's been out of the water for 10 to 15 minutes the shark will simmer down dramatically as its life begins to fade. But no matter how long a shark has been out of the water, anglers must be vigilant and careful around the head and jaws because even though the animal may be "dead" the nerves and muscles often react and cause the fish to bite.

Rolling a Shark Into the Boat

When anglers catch a large shark and don't have the equipment or man-power to get it aboard, they can sometimes avoid the time consuming towing method of getting it home by "rolling" the fish into the boat. To accomplish this, anglers will need to first use the tail rope to pull the aft-end of the shark as high out of the water as possible and tie it off to a spring-line cleat. Then, with the boat moving ahead slowly, they should take the head rope back to the stern-cleat on the same side, pull it very tight (effectively stretching the shark between the two cleats) and tie it off. One end of a third and rather long rope (the "rolling line") should now be tied to the stern cleat on the opposite side of the boat, brought back across the deck, passed down the side of the boat between the hull and the shark, looped under the midsection of the shark, and then brought back into the boat.

With the boat moving ahead to provide additional buoyancy of both shark and boat, the free end of the rolling line is then pulled in by as many crewmembers as possible. Because this line passes around the shark, as it's tightened it will roll the fish up the side of the boat, over the gunwale and onto the deck. This technique won't work for all boat configurations and really large sharks can still be problem, but in a lot of cases it's just the ticket for getting a shark aboard for the ride home. Anglers just need to be extra careful that they don't put too much weight on one side and swamp their boat in the process. Remember: the idea is to bring the shark up and into the boat, not sink the boat down around the shark. Also, be warned that rolling a rough-skinned shark up the side of a boat doesn't do the glossy gel-coat any favors.

A little trick we came up with to prevent unfortunate incidents while loading sharks is to put a bucket over their head. While the shark is still hanging over the side of the boat we pass the head rope through the handle of a plastic bucket which is then pushed up over the shark's head like a helmet and held in place by tension on the head rope. With the bucket over its head the shark can't bite anything in the boat and is a lot safer to have as a shipmate for the ride home! A standard five-gallon bucket works great for all but the biggest makos, threshers, lemons, spinners, and blacktips, but anglers will need something bigger for wide headed sharks such as hammerheads, tigers, and bulls.

Releasing Sharks

One of the dirty little secrets of recreational fishermen is that there are those among our ranks that don't care a thing about any fish that's not destined to come home with them in their cooler or on their boat. They fish only for food and egotistical bragging rights and have absolutely no concern for the welfare of any fish they hook that's either the wrong size or species to keep. Fortunately, most recreational anglers recognize that the fish they release today represent the best hopes for the future of the species and of their sport, and need to be fought, handled, and released properly to ensure their best chance for survival.

Within some fisheries anglers might find that they have the opportunity to release very few, if any, of the fish they catch. But due to the physical size and abundance of many shark species, along with the variations in edibility and quality of their meat, and certainly because of many state and federal catch regulations, shark fishermen end up releasing far more sharks than they ever bring home. Therefore, anglers must have a good understanding of how to release a shark so that both fish and fisherman part company none the worse for the encounter.

No less than if the shark is going to be boated, to properly release a shark requires planning, equipment, commitment, and a coordinated effort by angler and crew. The goal should be to bring the shark to the boat "tired" but not totally exhausted by the fight, and then free the fish by either clipping the leader as close to the shark as possible or to use a de-hooking tool to remove the hook. Of course, during the process anglers will likely wish to snap a few photos and possibly tag the shark before it is sent on it's way, all of which is fine providing it's done in a both a safe and timely manner.

As described earlier, the first order of business will be for the mate to grab the leader and get control of the shark beside the boat. When a shark comes to the boat time is of the essence, and anglers need to take care of business within a few short minutes to ensure a healthy release and not to increase the odds that the fish does something stupid and ends up wrapping the line or leader around the propeller or rudder. Keeping the boat slowly moving ahead during the release process will help the mate to keep control of the shark and also help to keep the fish healthy by maintaining a flow of water over its gills. A moving boat can also be better for photographs as the shark will be laid out on the surface and the skipper can move the boat so that the sun is at the best angle.

When it's finally time to say "bye-bye" most anglers will simply reach down as close as possible to the business end of the shark and snip the leader with a good set of wire-cutters or angler pliers.

Scalloped hammerhead numbers are down, so even though it was legal to keep this shark, the "right" thing to do was to release it.

While I don't want anyone to get hurt, I will suggest that fishermen make the effort to cut the leader as close to the shark (jaws) as possible. If you have to leave a hook in the poor critter the least you can do is get as much of the leader off of it as possible. Until the hook rusts away the shark doesn't need to have a few feet of heavy leader protruding from its mouth and possibly tangling up with objects it's feeding on or swimming around.

Cut the leader close but be careful, we once had a 100 pound sandbar shark up to the boat that we had caught on a two-hook rig. The shark was on the bottom hook and the top hook was a foot above the shark's head, which my mate was holding above the water by the leader. As I bent over the transom to cut the leader between

With the shark close to the boat, the release can be as simple as clipping the leader as close as possible.

the hooks, the shark started shaking its head and managed to imbed the top 14/0 hook in my upper arm. Now attached to the shark, all I could do was look up at my mate and say "don't let go!" Thankfully he held tight until another crewmember was able to cut the shark free. Sharking is exciting enough; no one needs to add to the thrill by getting into trouble like that!

Now that I've explained how to release a shark by cutting the leader I'd better fess up and say that we almost never do that anymore. It used to be that every time we released a shark we lost a hook, now we get almost every hook back, which is better for us because we don't have to buy so many hooks, and better for the sharks because it lessens the chance that the hooks could cause problems before they dissolve away. The ARC (aquatic release conservation) De-hooker is an incredible tool that's designed to safely remove a hook from a fish of almost any size or type and in some cases even if that hook has been swallowed. This tool comes in various sizes and is basically a stainless steel rod with a blunt corkscrew-like bend at one end and a handle at the other.

To use the ARC De-hooker, the person holding the leader slips the loop at the end of the tool around the leader and then slides it down the leader to the bend of the hook. Then, while keeping tension on the leader with one hand, the de-hooker is pushed down in a hard and fast motion to dislodge the hook. The secret and real beauty of this tool is the design and special bend of the loop that after it pops the hook out it protects the point from re-hooking the fish on the way out.

This is what allows it to even remove hooks that have been swallowed and are lodged in the fish's stomach. However, our own research has revealed that this tool should not be used on the rare occasions when a circle hook is set in the throat or stomach as it will tear too mush tissue during extraction.

While its known that hooks left in saltwater fish will quickly corrode away and usually create no ill effects on the fish, it has also been shown that when it's possible to remove a hook without creating any undue stress or trauma it will further increase the chances that the fish will survive. The ARC De-hooker is a must-have tool for every fisherman particularly those who participate in fisheries that

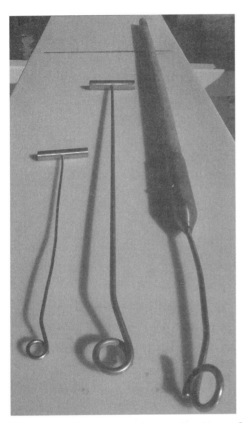

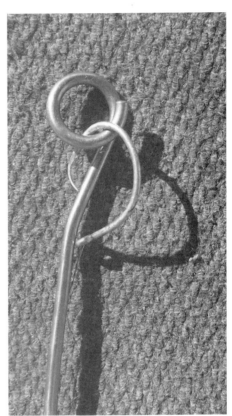

The simple yet unique design of the ARC De-hooker prevents the hook from rehooking the fish after extraction.

ARC De-hookers come in a variety of sizes and work for all kinds of fish.

have a high rate of catch-and-release such as with sharks.

Tagging

Those who get a little experience under their belts and wish to take their shark fishing to another level often sign-up to participate in the National Marine Fisheries Service (NMFS) Cooperative Shark Tagging Program. Through this government program, anglers receive shark tags and instructions on how to use them. The tags themselves have a stainless steel dart that fits on the insertion needle at the end of a tag-stick. From the deck, the tagger is able to insert the dart just under the skin of a shark while it's still in the water. Attached to the dart by a few inches of heavy monofilament line is a Plexiglas capsule containing a message written in English, Spanish, French, Japanese, and Norwegian with instructions to notify NMFS if the shark is recaptured.

The tags are provided to fishermen free of charge and are attached to self-addressed post cards. After implanting the tag, anglers fill out the cards with details about species, location, length, weight, sex and overall condition. If the shark is recaptured the NMFS sends the original tagger, and the person who recaptured the shark, information about where, when, and how the fish was caught along with details about how much it grew during its time at liberty.

Anglers who accept the responsibility of tagging any type of fish must keep in mind that tagging is not a "game" that can be done haphazardly. Tagging programs are established to help provide biologists and marine managers with a variety of important data that they'll use to further their studies and provide better management options. The data derived from a tagged shark will be of little use if the tagger misidentifies the species or provides other information that is inaccurate. It's also counter-productive if the shark is tagged in such a way that the tag or tagging process causes injury to the animal.

Before a shark is brought to the boat the tag-stick should be ready and everyone aboard must know their duties, including: someone to wire the fish, someone to plant the tag, and someone to record the information. When the shark is wired alongside the boat, the first goal should be to observe as many details as possible about the animal and record its species, estimated length and weight, overall condition (good, very weak, gut hooked, evidence of current or healed-over injuries, etc.) and the sex of the shark.

Most of this information is pretty easy to obtain except the sex part. With a dead shark it's easy to look for the presence or absence of claspers behind the pelvic fins and know that it's a male if it has them and a female if it doesn't. But I guess some sharks are just a little more modest than others because a live shark on the wire is not always so willing to roll over and show its private parts to the nice folks up in the boat, thus requiring the wire-man to work the shark back and forth through the water in effort to get it to roll over long enough for a quick peek. The hardest sharks to sex are immature males because their claspers will not have grown long enough to project beyond the two pelvic fins and are, therefore, hard to see if the shark doesn't roll over and remain still for a second or two. If the process of sexing an uncooperative shark requires too much effort and risks injury to the animal, it's better just to indicate "sex unknown" on the tag card and leave it at that.

Of course, planting the tag on the shark is a critical step in the process that shouldn't be rushed. Tags are to be placed just below the dorsal fin and angled so that they stream back. This requires that the tagger be located slightly above, behind, and to one side of the shark as he plants the tag. It also requires that the person wiring the shark is able to maneuver the animal in such a way that the gives the tagger the necessary angle needed for a good tag shot. Just jabbing a tag any-old place on a fish is likely to do more harm than good, particularly if the tag enters the head, gill, or body cavity area. Blue sharks are probably the worst, but any shark that wants to twist or roll while it's being held at the boat by the leader will require patience, good timing, and some marksmanship on behalf of the tagger.

Over the years, sharks we've tagged off the Mid-Atlantic region have been recaptured off the coast of Cuba, Mexico, South America, Canada, Spain, the Azores, and every state along the East Coast and Gulf of Mexico. I've had sharks recaptured after being at liberty for as long as 12 years and as short as just a few hours. On two occasions we caught a tiger shark in the morning and the same fish that afternoon—I guess tigers aren't the quickest learners in fish school! The tag from a spinner shark we caught off Maryland ended up being recovered nine years later at a fish market in Baltimore, after the commercial fishermen who caught the shark off North Carolina sent the carcass off to market tag and all. The strangest return I had was that of a blue shark we tagged that when recaptured aboard a commercial vessel was reported to be a yellowfin tuna! Unless somehow by metamorphosis that shark turned into a tuna I'm thinking that the fishermen on that boat might need to brush-up on their fish ID. Needless to say some of these sharks really get around, and it's always interesting and very gratifying to get notice of a tag return.

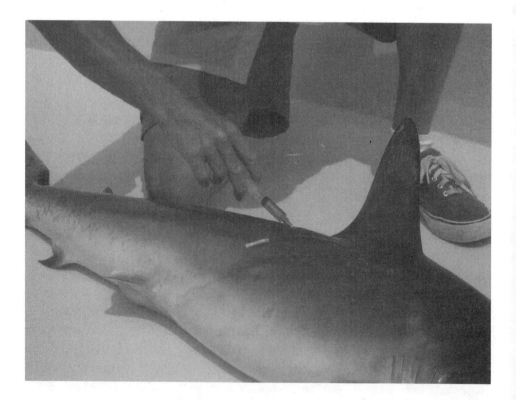

To assist biologists in scientific research on sharks, I inject a smooth hammerhead with Oxytetracycline.

In addition to a tag, most sharks we catch get a dose of Oxy-tetracycline which is an antibiotic that, as a side effect, stains the vertebra of the shark. Years later, if the shark is ever recaptured and biologists are able to examine the vertebra they can measure how much it grew since the original capture and staining. This data will eventually allow biologists to determine the age of sharks simply by measuring the vertebra.

Sharkers wishing to volunteer for the shark-tagging program should contact:

Apex Predators Investigation
NOAA/NMFS/NEFSC
28 Tarzwell Drive
Narragansett, RI 02882-1152 USA
401-782-3200
http://na.nefsc.noaa.gov/sharks/

Guns

You may have noticed that in the preceding descriptions of techniques for landing sharks, nowhere did I mention anything about shooting a shark. That wasn't a mistake, I left it out because as far as I'm concerned there is absolutely zero reason to shoot a shark before boating it. In more than three decades of sharking I have never encountered a situation where I thought it would be prudent to shoot a shark. I have plenty of guns back home, but save them for the woods and marshes and have no need to keep one on the boat. I know that for a lot of shark fishermen it's standard procedure to shoot their catch before bringing it aboard, and I've surely heard all the arguments in favor of doing so, most of which center around the safety factor for the crew or that anglers don't want a shark tearing up the inside of their boat.

Maybe I've just been really lucky all these years, but after safely dealing with thousands of sharks ranging in sizes from less than 10 to over 1,000 pounds aboard boats from 14 to 60 feet with nothing more than flying gaffs, tail ropes, and tag sticks, I know from experience that the techniques I've described are both safe and effective.

CHAPTER 11

Safety

Some folks consider shark fishing to be a sport with a lot of inherent dangers, none the least of which would be of the "hunter" suddenly becoming the "hunted" and getting eaten by his prey. How can we forget the ending of the movie *JAWS* when the great white sucks Captain Quint out of the cockpit of his boat, like someone slurping an oyster off the half-shell? But despite the fact that a lot of folks who know nothing about shark fishing will sometimes try and paint shark fishermen as macho thrill seekers who put their life on the line

Stay away from the business end of the shark!

to battle deadly monsters of the sea, in reality, as long as you stay out of the water and keep your body parts out of a shark's mouth, the sport is no more dangerous than most other types of offshore big game fishing.

Sharks in the movies have been portrayed as vengeful villains that attack boats in effort to devour the tasty crew one by one. But thankfully this ain't Hollywood, and sharks don't necessarily even know that there's a buffet of human protein aboard the big floating object with the chum bucket hanging off its transom. I'm not trying to be demeaning to these marvelous predators when I say that sharks swimming about a chum slick are just big lugs following their senses to what might be their next meal. Unless you do something stupid like climbing down into the tiger cage, visiting the zoo is usually safe for the whole family. And so is shark fishing, as long as you follow a few precautions, don't do anything stupid, and by all means stay in the boat.

Sharks are not out to get us, in fact they're really out to get away from us, and therein lies much of the inherent danger of shark fishing. Most of the hazards involved with the sport are not so much because anglers are dealing specifically with sharks as much as they're dealing with big fish that are bound and determined not to do what the fishermen want them to. Harness someone up to a monster billfish or a giant tuna on heavy tackle and you better make sure nothing goes awry or that angler could end up "swimming with the fishes" really quick! The same holds true at boat-side when trying to wire or gaff one of those more "harmless" fish. Even if it were stone-cold dead, just trying to hang on to 700 pounds of any kind of fish beside a boat poses some hazards; add a little life to the critter and there's all the more reason for caution. Since shark anglers are more likely to encounter situations where they must deal with larger than average fish, they're going to have to exhibit an extra measure of caution more often than other fishermen—a burden they must not become complacent about.

Don't let them jump in the boat!

The first big mako I ever hooked picked up a bait and launched about eight feet into air the second I set the hook. In fact it jumped eight times in a row before throwing the hook. Later in the day we hooked a small mako and, while fighting it, brought in the other lines. Unfortunately we only brought those lines to the boat, not in the boat... and a 270 pounder snuck in and grabbed a bait that was left hanging in the water. Remembering the way the shark reacted earlier in the morning, and not wanting to have eight feet of fresh mako join us too soon in our 19 foot boat, we opted not to set the hook until it moved away from the boat. But the shark wouldn't go anywhere, it just kept swimming circles under the boat. So we did the next best thing; since it wouldn't leave us we started up the engine and left it. Once we got about 50 yards away we threw the reel in gear, set the hook, and the

Wisely, Steve Gladmon stayed at the "safe-end" of this shark until he slid it back into the water.

fight was on!

As it was, that mako didn't jump as soon as it felt the hook, but after seeing what we saw earlier in the morning we weren't about to take the chance. That was many years ago, but since then we've always made it a habit to try not to hook makos close to the boat. A few hundred pounds of jumping fish is a sight to behold, but it's also kind of scary to think of the consequences should so much weight come crashing down into a boat. If you read enough shark books you're liable to come away with the notion that the jumping abilities of makos has them landing in boats all the time. I haven't met anyone who made claim that it happened to them, and while I've been splashed a lot of times, I'm glad to say that no makos have chosen such an impromptu way to board my boat yet, and that's okay with me!

While I expect that a lot of the stories we hear or read about "crash landings" are more fiction than fact, sharkers do need to be careful whenever they have any of the known jumpers such as makos, threshers, spinners, blacktips, and even great whites, close to the boat. This concern reinforces the reasons to make sure a shark is properly tired-out by the angler before trying to deal with it close to the boat.

Clean Up the Clutter

A friend of mine was hooked up and fighting a big shark that made a dash for the for the other side of the boat, and as he tried to follow by squeezing around the console, he got his foot tangled in a wire leader that was left in a pile on the deck. On his next step the leader pulled tight around his ankle and drove a 12/0 hook in past the barb. Another fisherman I know managed to imbed a 14/0 hook right through the back of his knee as he was coming down a flying bridge ladder–someone had haphazardly hung a two-hook shark rig on the ladder step.

Experienced anglers come to know that, in less than a second, life aboard a fishing boat can go from very boring to pure chaos with the actions and reactions of everyone aboard possibly meaning the difference between landing or losing the fish of a lifetime. With all the craziness that goes on during a typical fight with a shark, no one should have to worry about tripping over, tangling with, or slipping on anything aboard the boat that can (and should) be stowed out of the way. Clean and orderly boats always make for a better and safer platform to fish from.

Wiring a Shark

One of the most dangerous duties preformed while shark fishing is when someone (usually the mate) grabs the leader in order to control the shark at the boat side long enough to gaff or release the fish. When the leader is first taken in hand a shark will often respond to the extra pressure by shaking its head a few times and then mustering up enough energy to make another run away form the boat. I know I stated this earlier but it can not be stressed enough: even if the shark only weighs a couple hundred pounds, a mate is not going to be able to hold it back if it really wants to get away from the boat, so he must always be able to quickly release his hold on the leader and allow it to slip freely from his hands. If the mate does not, or cannot release his hold; the leader will break, the hook will pull free, or he's going swimming!

Obviously, none of those options are acceptable, and the entire crew must work together to ensure that none of them occur. As the leader is brought in the excess should be deposited back overboard so there is little chance it will snag on the deck, or that anyone might step on or tangle with it. Adding a second set of hands only increases the chance for a mishap so the wiring of a fish must only be done by one person. During this process the angler must also take care not to move the rod tip in any direction that would allow the excess leader to tangle around anything.

It's not uncommon to have a hand on the wire many times before the shark is finally whipped enough that the mate can hold on and finally control the fish beside the boat. This process cannot be rushed without increasing the chances for a lost fish or an injured crewmember.

Sharks don't attack, they respond.

We can tell when a dog is frightened because it will tuck its tail, droop its ears, hunch its back, and cower, or if it's ready to fight it will bristle its back, bare its teeth and growl. Sharks, like most fish, can't do any of that. No matter what condition or mood they're in, they always look the same. And since there's no way to look at a shark and tell if it's full of energy or ready to die, anglers must always be extremely cautious. For most folks, close quarters work with sharks will involve the process of securing the head or tail ropes, loading and unloading the animals in and out of the boat, and maybe securing them in the boat for the ride home. But sometimes anglers need to get a little more "up close and personal" with a shark in order to take care of some sort of situation such as when a shark comes in all wrapped-up in the leader and needs to be unwound before being released, or a shark that for one reason or the other needs to be measured in the water before release. Such tasks can have anglers hanging over the side of the boat and holding on to the shark's tail or fins and trying not to get bit or slapped in the process. It can be dicey work, but can certainly be done without incident if anglers maintain an escape route, know how a shark can move, and keep their own body parts out of the danger zone.

Whether it's being held by a gaff line, tail rope, or just on the leader, a shark at the boat can be a kicking, rolling, snapping machine. But anglers need to be aware that sharks at the boat side don't react this way because they're mean and just want to get a piece of the crew. It might be hard to comprehend but you've got to figure that when put in that predicament even the biggest and baddest shark out there is going to be in fear for its life, not understanding what's going on, and just doing what it can to get away. Since the only two resources sharks have to get themselves out of trouble are their teeth and their tails, all they know to do when threatened is to snap their teeth and kick their tails. As long as angler can stay away from colliding with either of those two parts they should fair pretty well.

Whether it's at the side of the boat or on the deck, folks will find that when in trouble, sharks often swing their heads from side to side and blindly bite at whatever their jaws come in contact with. They might turn to bite at something that's touching their sides or messing with their tail, but they don't see something (or someone), recognize it as a threat, and then go after it. Put a live shark on the deck and it will kick its tail and swing its head around until it finally finds something to clamp its jaws down on, whether that's a cushion, a chair pedestal, a cooler handle, or an arm—but it won't spot the crew, recognize them as the source of their peril, and specifically try to bite them.

While knowledge of this won't make a shark any safer to handle, it should give fishermen at least a thread of confidence to know that they can indeed do some work on sharks without being targeted or bitten by the animal as long as they stay clear of the danger zone surrounding the jaws. Since sharks cannot bend their bodies up or down, this danger zone is an arch on either side of the head. How far to either side they can go depends upon the shark species, as some are more flexible then others. For instance; sandtigers and blue sharks can turn around far enough to just about bite the base of their own tails, thus giving them a 180 degree danger zone on either side, while makos and threshers are more rigid in the body and can only get around about 90 degrees to a side. Most other sharks can bend somewhere between those two ranges—close to the tail but not quite to it. It's good to know that stuff when you're trying to get a rope on or off the tail of a shark that's not in the best of moods!

Grabbing the Tail

It's one thing to control a shark with the aid of a tail rope; it's a whole other story trying to do so by holding on to the tail. I'll cut right to the chase on this one and say, DON'T EVER try to hold a shark by the tail! If it's a fair size shark that's still in the water it will slap your face harder than your ex-girlfriend ever did, and if the fish is on deck it will throw you across the cockpit. But those injuries will be minor compared to what can happen with small sharks.

Anglers will often catch little three to four foot sharks such as duskies, sharpnose, spinners or other species that (even though they're small) still have a full set of very sharp teeth. While these sharks are usually released, because they're small, anglers often choose to bring them aboard to get the hook out or maybe pose them for a photo before returning them to the water. In the process, folks sometimes choose to lift and hold these sharks by their tail. Bad idea, pick a healthy little shark up by the tail and its head is going to start twisting, swinging, and snapping. No problem on the out-swing, but on the in-swing those snapping jaws are going to contact the angler somewhere between the waist and knee. And a bite in the wrong place from a 15 to 20 pounder can kill you just as dead as one from a big shark.

Small sharks can be safely picked up by adults (NOT children) with one hand around the base of the tail and the other one firmly gripping the shark behind the head or under the belly just behind the pectoral fins. Holding a small shark should only be attempted if the fish is calm and not struggling. If the shark starts going nuts while it's being held it should be quickly put down or back overboard, but don't drop the poor thing on the deck. It's amazing how strong these animals are, even a little four-footer cannot be restrained by hand, and it's unwise to even make the attempt. If a shark is raising a ruckus on deck just leave it alone and work on moving tackle and equipment out of its way until it calms down, which it will do in a very short time.

Skin and Tails

Look closely at shark skin with a magnifying glass and instead of scales one will see what appears to be very tiny overlapping teeth all pointing back toward the tail. These "dermal denticals" (skin teeth) are what makes sharks feel relatively smooth if you rub them from head to tail but very rough when rubbed from tail to head. Like different grit sandpaper, some species of sharks are rougher than others. For instance makos and threshers have some smoothest textured skin of the sharks while tiger and nurse sharks have some of the roughest.

This rough skin doesn't make life any easier for those who must work closely with sharks, particularly when securing a tail-rope and the fish slaps your forearms or face, or when a shark on the deck smacks you a good one to the back of your legs. It's kind of like getting whacked by a yardstick with sandpaper wrapped around it–ouch! Such injuries will rarely draw blood and they certainly won't be life threatening, but like a painful sunburn, the effects will be felt for a couple days after the encounter.

Obviously it's important to be very careful around the front end of a shark, but fishermen better know that the stern half is certainly not hazard-free. Compared to most fish, sharks have very long tails, which when flailing about beside a boat can deliver quite a blow, in some cases actually fracturing bones or causing lacerations to unlucky crewmembers within reach. Anglers must be extra cautious not to allow hands, arms, or heads to get caught between the shark and the side of the boat or the gunwale.

No discussion of the dangers of shark tails can be complete

A slap from the tail of a small thresher like this may only sting a bit, but a larger animal can inflict serious injuries.

without addressing threshers. While it may not look rigid enough to hurt anyone, the extra long top lobe of a thresher tail is absolutely something anglers need to wary of. Just a little bit of movement by the shark at the base of its tail translates to a whip-effect out toward the tip. The tail might look somewhat flimsy, but the entire leading edge is extremely hard, and when that edge strikes something it does so not with a simple "slap" (like from the side of a yardstick) but with a powerful "punch" (like from the edge of a yardstick).

There's an old story about a fisherman off Florida whose de-capitated body was found in his boat. The story has it that somehow folks figured the unfortunate fellow was looking over the side of his vessel when a thresher's tail whipped up and took his head off! I

You don't want to be whacked by a tail of these proportions!

know fishermen who required a few stitches after getting whacked in the arms by threshers, and I've got a couple scars on my legs from too-close encounters with thresher tails—I even had a tail take my hat and sunglasses off—but I think it's a real stretch to think that they could actually knock someone's head off...but it does make for a good story!

Sharks Never Really Die

I once brought a bag of steaks home from a shark that had been caught earlier in the day. I emptied the bag in the kitchen sink with the intention to wrap some of the meat for the freezer and cook the rest for dinner. The shark had been boated at about 1:00, cleaned and bagged up at 4:30, and at 7:00 in the evening the meat was lay-ing in my sink, quivering and twitching like something from a horror movie. My wife had seen the occurrence before, but we had a couple houseguests who were a little skeptical about what we planned to serve-up for dinner that night.

Obviously, that shark was deader than dead, and had been for some time, but the key thing here is that the nerves in the meat con-tinued to fire off and make the muscles contract long after the shark had "clinically" expired. Anglers often wish to know, "how long until the shark is dead?" because they want to get in close to the jaws and start poking at the teeth or maybe pull their hook out. If the steaks are still twitching six hours after the shark was pulled out of the water, when will it be safe to put a hand inside a shark's mouth? My answer would be that it is never safe to assume that a shark is dead enough not to be wary around the teeth and jaws.

In my years working on the docks and as weigh-master at shark tournaments I've repeatedly witnessed the astonishment of crews when they see a shark they brought in that "hasn't moved for hours" suddenly bite-down on a gaff or head rope they're using to unload their catch. I once watched as a vacationer waddled up to a big tiger shark that was hanging, handed a camera to his wife and said, "honey, when I stick my head in its mouth you take the picture." He wasn't too happy with me when I interfered with his photo-op by telling him that if he proceeded with his plan he could lose his head, or at the very least need to wear a toupee for the rest of his life. But he wasn't quite so upset with me when he saw the jaws snap shut on a mop handle I stuck in the shark's mouth!

I've seen shark carcasses still kicking more than an hour after the head and guts were removed, just as I've seen shark heads still snapping long after they've been separated from the body. All of which reinforces my conviction that shooting a shark does nothing to make it safe to be around and, therefore, why do it in the first place and possibly create a false sense of security?

Never assume that a shark is totally safe until it's cut-up and in the freezer, even then you'd better be careful when you open the door to grab a half gallon of ice-cream—you just never know! A friend of mine kept a twelve foot tiger shark in a walk-in freezer for three years until the biologists who requested it were ready for it. When it was time to move the shark out of the freezer my friend stood in front, grabbed it just under the snout and tried to lift and slide the animal to the side, he didn't realize his fingers had slipped inside the mouth and were gripping around the teeth until it was too late. The shark never got out of the freezer that day but my friend spent the rest of it in the hospital getting his hands sewn back together. Alive, dead, or in Popsicle form, never trust a shark.

CHAPTER 12

Harvesting and Eating Sharks

Some sharks are absolutely delicious. But unless anglers end up marooned and starving on a deserted Island, they'll find the best bet is to leave some sharks in the water rather than try to wrangle them onto a dinner plate. The difference between what's good to eat and what's not is dictated by both the species and the size of the shark. There are also a few species that might be good to eat, but are on the NMFS Prohibited Species List and therefore may not be boated anyway. It's the responsibility of every ethical fisherman to know which are worth bringing home and which are only candidates for catch-and-release before they boat or injure a shark in any way. Gaffing and tail roping a shark and then calling a buddy on the radio to ask if it's any good to eat doesn't cut it these days!

Anglers also need to know that most really large sharks are rarely very good to eat; this includes some of the more popular sharks like makos and threshers. Those two species, for instance, are excellent in the 100 to 300 pound range, but larger than that and they start to get tough and lose flavor. When makos and threshers grow over 400 or 500 pounds I don't consider them fit to eat at all. Of course, most fishermen dream of someday "bringing home the big one" which makes it understandably tough to release a once in a lifetime shark of those proportions—but it's awfully hard to justify killing such a animal if it only results in a few photos at the dock and coolers full of meat that no one wants to eat!

So, exactly what is the edibility list? Along with what I've learned from personal experience I've interviewed others, yet only managed to drum up conflicting opinions about the taste of certain species. Therefore, the following list is strictly from my own taste buds. Obviously, since we all have our own likes and dislikes, what's tasty to me might not be so appetizing to others. Also, I'm not including any sharks presently listed on the NMFS Prohibited Species List (which could change after the printing of this book) because whether they are good to eat or not they cannot be taken, so the issue is moot.

Mako—Excellent
Thresher—Excellent, sometimes better than mako
Blacktip—Very Good
Spinner—Very Good
Smooth Hammerhead—Good, must be bled and iced down quickly
Scalloped Hammerhead—Fair, must be bled and iced down quickly
Great Hammerhead—Poor, tough and flavorless
Atlantic Sharpnose—Excellent
Blue—Poor, mushy and requires a lot of preparation to make it palat-
able
Spiny Dogfish—Very Good, perfect for batter-fry cooking
Smooth Dogfish—Very Good
Tiger—Poor, tough and flavorless

Makos have long been known as a fine tasting shark.

Cleaning a Shark

Cleaning a shark can be as easy or as difficult as someone wants to make it. One evening I was strolling the charter docks down in Key West. It was late enough that the boats were all in, cleaned up, and the captains and crews had headed home for the night. No one was around except a couple guys who had been out fishing on one of the boats that day. They had brought home a 100 pound bull shark. Apparently they got off the boat, told the captain they'd be back to take care of their shark, and then scooted off to a local bar for a "few" drinks.

When I happened upon the scene, the shark was hanging by its tail from one of the dock's fish racks. It had obviously been there a while because in the 80-degree heat its skin was dry as a bone and wrinkled like an old man. With beer cans in one hand and Buck skinning knifes in the other, the two rather portly fellows, both sporting jeans, no shirt, bad sunburns, and very full beards, didn't quite look like they knew where to start as they gently swayed back and forth in their black leather biker-boots.

Finally, one of the guys pinched up a bit of skin on one side just below the tail and started cutting. He wrestled off about a two by five inch strip of skin, threw it down on the dock, stepped back, took a couple slugs from his beer, stepped up to the shark, shaved another piece off, flicked it on the dock, then turned to his buddy and said, "this ain't like skinning no deer, we're gonna be here all night!"

Maybe they were going to be there all night, but I surely wasn't. As I walked away I couldn't help but laugh at the image of what the captain might find the next morning when he returned to his boat. I could see the two guys passed out on the nearby picnic table, the shark head and guts piled in a nearby trashcan, and the dock littered with beer cans, little scraps of shark skin dried to the dock, the palm trees, and the transom of the closest boat. Like I said, cleaning a shark can be as easy or as difficult as someone wants to make it, they chose the latter.

It's important to clean a shark in a timely manner. From the time a shark comes out of the water, unless it can go directly on ice it's a race with time to get the animal cleaned and in a cooler before the meat starts to turn. Anglers must not put off cleaning their catch too long after returning to the dock. If the carcass is allowed to warm up the blood will break down and permit toxins to taint the meat, giving it a very strong ammonia smell. This ammonia smell will stay with the shark meat even after it's been frozen; fortunately it can be neutralized later by soaking the meat in milk or lemon juice, but it's far better not to allow the meat to be tainted in the first place.

The very best way to handle a shark is to cut its head off, gut it, and put it on ice right away. Of course that's not always possible, or desirable for anglers who would like to weigh the entire shark at the dock. Besides, very few of even the best equipped boats will have fish boxes or even fish bags large enough for really big sharks.

Keeping in mind that the main problems come from warm meat and blood, anglers can start by keeping a shark relatively cool by leaving it in the water until they are ready to head home, they can also bleed the shark while it's hanging in the water by cutting a gash just in front of the tail on the underside. For the ride back to the dock

----

Professional fish cleaner Rose Stivers proves that a sharp knife and proper techniques are more important than size when it comes to whittling a shark down to edible steaks.

fishermen should cover the fish with wet towels, and if possible surround it with ice.

The process of cleaning a shark is not too much different from that of other types of large fish; some of it is a lot easier and some a little harder. The harder part is dealing with the skin, which is so tough it can dull a knife's blade before you get halfway through the critter. And like the Key West fishermen found out, sharks don't skin like a deer, a moose, a snake, or a catfish! The skin of a shark will not just pull off the meat, it must be cut off–but NOT with a hunting knife a little bit at a time!

What makes cleaning a shark easier than other large fish is that there are no bones to carve around, just one vertebrae of cartilage (no ribs) running fore and aft. Other than that the animal is head, meat, guts, skin, and fin. Anglers can save themselves some trouble if before they transfer the animal from the scale or hoist it to the cleaning table, they first put a large trashcan under it and then gut the shark by opening it from vent to gills and cut free what's necessary to let all the innards fall into the can. Then, starting just behind the pectoral fins and angling forward, a circular cut should be made around the shark's head and fins all the way down to the vertebrae. A serrated knife should be used to cut through the vertebrae and allow the head to fall into the bucket.

While the carcass is still hanging, it's convenient to cut the remaining fins off before transferring it to the cleaning table. Once it's all up on the table the tail can be removed by cutting around the base and then snapping or cutting the vertebrae. Before filleting, if the carcass is more than about four feet long, it usually helps to cut it in half or into as many pieces as necessary to render it down to manageable size. Now, each piece may be filleted by starting at the back and slicing to the belly.

Particularly with large sharks, the fillets themselves are often quite wide, requiring that they be cut in half lengthwise so that the final steaks are not too large. The fillets (or "loins") can then be skinned by laying the fillet skin-side down on the table and slicing the meat free. Once skinned, all fillets can be crosscut into steaks of about three-quarters of an inch.

While cleaning a shark, a little trick to help maintain the edge of a knife is to always try to cut the skin from the inside out. This prevents the blade from being dulled as it's drawn across the hard dermal denticles on the outside of the skin.

Provided that it's wrapped properly, anglers will find that shark meat keeps quite well in a freezer. Like anything that goes into the freezer the primary objective should be to eliminate the opportunity for air to reach the meat and create freezer-burn. Vacuum-bagging is one of the best methods to prepare meat for a freezer, but it requires that one has access to the proper equipment to do so. The next best technique that I've found is to tightly double-wrap the meat in plastic wrap and then put it inside a zipper-lock style freezer bag.

Recipes

Shark meat is not oily or strong and can be cooked-up just about any fashion people like to cook fish. The firm texture lends itself perfectly to just about any kind of grilling technique someone might want to throw at it. While I really like smoked fish, I've got to say that I've never been a big fan of smoked shark, it just doesn't seem to have the right flavor for it. The following are just a few simple recipes we enjoy back home.

Quick & Healthy Roland Meade "Microwave Shark"

My friend Roland Meade introduced me to this recipe that's fast, simple and works for all kind of fish, and it's also particularly good for black seabass.

Ingredients:
Two shark steaks (or other fish)
Butter or Margarine
Old Bay Seasoning
Fresh Lemon

Slice steaks (across the grain) into half-inch thick "fish-fingers," and place the meat in a glass baking dish. Melt the butter or margarine and pour it over meat. Sprinkle with Old Bay Seasoning (a lot or a little). Cover the dish tightly with plastic wrap, then microwave it on high for 3 to 4 minutes just until fish is white inside. Sprinkle with fresh lemon juice just before serving

Mako Pinwheels

I'll take credit for inventing this recipe. I got the idea after watching bakers make cinnamon-rolls. You can really "wow" your friends with this one because it looks as good as it tastes and it's really not that much work.

Ingredients:

2-3 lb. Loin of Mako
Butter or Margarine
Pack of chopped frozen spinach (thawed and drained)
6-8 slices of Provolone cheese
1 pkg. Knorr Hollandaise Sauce (make package directions)
Fresh squeezed lemon juice

Lay the mako loin on a large cutting surface. Turn your knife sideways and start slicing (against the grain) a half-inch from the bottom of the meat while rolling the loin away from the knife. Imagine the loin is a roll of paper and you're slicing a long string of sheets from the roll. This should result in a half-inch sheet of mako about 18 inches long and six inches wide. Smear the top side of meat with butter or Margarine, cover the top side of meat with spinach, then roll the meat back together to from a log. Hold the log together while slicing half-inch thick pinwheel-like steaks. Carefully slide the pinwheels onto a baking pan or cookie sheet, and broil on high (about 6" from broiler) until white and flaky (don't try to flip.) When it's nearly done, top the pinwheel with cheese and place it back in oven, just long enough to barely melt the cheese. Top with Hollandaise sauce and lemon juice.

Bluefish a'la Fish Finder

This can be used for sharks or almost any other type of fish, but it's particularly good for big bluefish. I include this recipe only because anglers often encounter a lot of bluefish while sharking, and quite frankly I'm sick and tied of hearing folks complain about how poor big bluefish are for eating–it ain't so! Try this recipe with even a big 12 to 14 pound chopper bluefish and you'll agree. Just don't make the mistake of ever freezing bluefish–eat them fresh or not at all.

Ingredients:

Fresh skinned bluefish fillets (cut into quarters)
Two large fresh sliced tomatoes
One large fresh sliced green pepper
One medium sweet fresh sliced onion
Grated Parmesan Cheese
Salt & Pepper

Layer a baking dish with onion, green pepper & tomato, then layer with the fillets. Next, layer again with vegetables, then layer again with fillets. Make the top layer with vegetables. Cover and bake at 400-degrees until fish can be flaked with a fork.

Lots of liquid will be made during baking; carefully drain off all this liquid. Remove the dish from the oven and sprinkle the top (liberally) with Parmesan cheese; return it to the oven, and bake uncovered for another two to three minutes. Drain off any more liquid, salt & pepper to taste, and serve with grated parmesan cheese and fresh lemon.

Mounting the Jaws

No shark should ever be killed just for its jaws. But there's clearly nothing wrong when an angler lands a shark for its meat and wishes to have the jaws to display as a lasting memory of the fish. Preparing a set of jaws for the wall is not an easy process, but it's not

Makos undoubtedly have some of the most impressive dentures.

so difficult that anyone with the time and the inclination shouldn't be able to accomplish it if they follow the relatively simple procedures.

The first thing to know about preparing shark jaws so that they turn out clean and white is that there is no easy shortcut. Folks must ignore what anyone might say about setting them on an ant-hill, hanging them in a tree, burying them in the ground, or hanging them off the dock and letting the minnows and crabs pick at them. And by all means, unless someone wants nothing more than a pot full of teeth they should not put the jaws in boiling water.

The most important thing to know about preparing shark jaws is that the teeth are only held to the jaw by a fleshy substance. In fact, the jaw itself is made of four segments of cartilage held together by the same substance. So any little critter, chemical, or drop of boiling water employed to remove tissue from the jaw is also going to remove the teeth from the jaw. And since hanging a set of jaws on

After the jaws are roughed-out and the inner teeth exposed, it then becomes a tedious process of picking and scraping.

the wall without any of the teeth doesn't quite project the true spirit of the shark, I wouldn't exactly recommend any of those cleaning techniques.

The tools I use to clean jaws include a small paring knife, a dinner spoon with one edge sharpened on a grinding wheel, some stainless steel wire, a couple three-eights inch wooden dowels, about a gallon of hydrogen peroxide, a knife sharpener, and a Kevlar fillet glove (sold in most tackle shops). The glove is quite important as it will keep the teeth from tearing the heck out of the hand holding the jaws throughout the process–I learned its value the hard way!

By feeling where they run under the skin, and then cutting around them, the jaws can be removed from the shark. Besides soft tissue they're not attached by much, just a little bit of cartilage at the top and at either side. Cutting too close will only increase the chances of cutting away at the jaw itself. Once the jaws are out of the fish

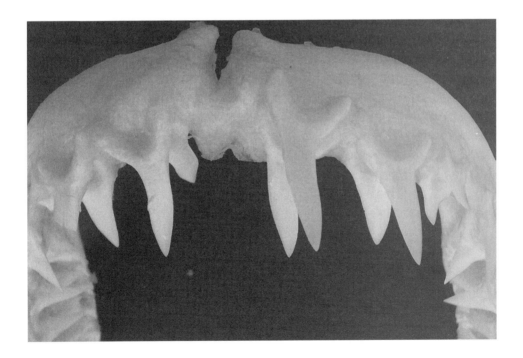

Soaking the jaws in hydrogen peroxide and water will help to whiten them.

they may be kept in a freezer for as long as needed until someone is ready to work on them.

After removal from the fish, the first step is to use the paring knife and remove all the large bits of skin and meat possible. One should keep a knife sharpener handy because the blade will constantly end up being drawn across the teeth and the edge won't last long. With all the "big stuff" removed it's then time to cut away the tissue that covers the inner rows of teeth. This is accomplished by working from the inside of the jaw and pushing the tip of the knife into the cavity where the inner rows of teeth reside and cutting back toward the corners of the jaw. This must be done for both the upper and lower sets of teeth.

With the inner teeth exposed it's time to start the tedious process of picking and scraping all the meat possible from the jaw. This is done with both the paring knife and the sharpened spoon and will take some time to complete. When all the meat possible is removed the jaws can be dipped in hot water to help loosen small bits of remaining tissue. Notice I said "dipped" in "hot" tap water, NOT left in boiling water! If the water is too hot and the jaws left in it too long (which can mean less than a minute) the entire set can be ruined.

After the "dipping" the jaws should be scraped some more, and when all the meat that can possibly be removed has been, they are ready to be soaked in a 50/50 solution of hydrogen peroxide and water. This soaking will whiten the jaws by dissolving away blood and it will help to loosen some of the very small bits of meat left after the scraping. The jaws may be soaked from 12 to 36 hours depending upon their size and how much blood needs to be removed.

After soaking, the jaws should be rinsed with fresh water and then scraped some more. When it's finally determined that nothing else can possibly come off of them, the jaws are finally ready for drying. They should now be opened to the desired position (kept "realistic" by not opening them too wide) and held in place with two wooden dowels, one holding them open, the other holding the proper width. The dowels are held to the jaws with the stainless wire.

Depending upon the size and thickness of the jaws, the drying time may take from three to more then seven days. It should not be attempted to dry jaws in areas of high humidity as they simply will

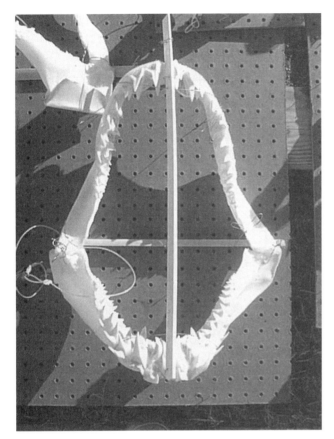

Finished jaws should be allowed to dry in an area free from, humidity, insects, and direct sunlight.

not dry out completely and may eventually start to attract insects and discolor. If it's hot and humid outside the jaws may be dried indoors in an air-conditioned space.

After drying, any small cracks that appear in the jaw should be filled with a white latex caulk, and then the entire jaw should be sealed with a couple light coats of a high quality polyurethane spray. The spray must not be applied too thick otherwise it will yellow the jaws over time.

Recreational shark fishing has transformed much over the past few decades. Much change has resulted from technological advances in boats, tackle, equipment, and a better understanding of the biology and habits of sharks. But I'd have to say that the big-

gest change has been in the attitudes and ethics of shark fishermen themselves. Sure, we like the jaws, but we're not going to kill
a shark for that purpose alone—and fewer sharks wind up hanging
by their tails at the dock these days. Certainly, much of this is due
to ever-tightening government regulations, but an increasing trend
among shark fishermen has many of them voluntarily practicing and
promoting standards of conservation that go beyond what is required
by law. Such ethical practices are absolutely essential if many shark
species are to survive after so many years of overexploitation.

Even during this era when many shark populations are at his-
toric lows, modern sharking can continue if participants within in the
fishery have the knowledge and commitment to fish responsibly and
never put their own ambitions before the well-being of the resource.
I hope you had as much fun reading this book as I had writing it. I
hope also that from it, you have gained not only a better understanding of how to catch sharks, but more importantly, a realistic respect
for these incredible predators.

BIOGRAPHY

As a child Mark Sampson grew up in a house filed with trophies and stories from his father's hunting safaris in Africa, India, and South America. Harold Sampson wasn't a fisherman, but he infected his son with a love of the outdoors and a desire to interact with some of God's larger creatures. Desire met opportunity when at age 13 Mark got a job working the docks at Bahia Marina in Ocean City, Maryland where he had the chance to fish offshore with many experienced captains.

As his interest and experience in shark fishing grew, in 1981 Mark and a few friends started the Ocean City Shark Sharkers Club and the Annual Ocean City Shark Tournament, an event which is still in existence today. In 1986 Mark (then "Captain Mark") took his passion for sharks one step farther when he bought his 40 foot *Fish Finder* and went into the charter fishing business full time. Naturally his specialty was (and still is) shark fishing.

But Mark's involvement in the recreational fishery has taken him far beyond his charter business. Since 1997 Mark has been a member of the NMFS Highly Migratory Species Advisory Panel, and since 2000 a member of the Maryland Sportfishing Advisory Commission. Both positions have allowed him the opportunity to work directly with fishery managers charged with the responsibility of managing and protecting this country's sharks and other marine resources.

A member of the Outdoor Writers Association of America, Mark has columns in the *Ocean Pines Independent, Daily Times,* and the *Fishing & Hunting Journal*. His freelance work also appears in other fishing, hunting, and outdoor related publications. This is his first book.

Since 1995 Mark has worked as volunteer for the National Aquarium in Baltimore's Marine Animal Rescue Program (MARP) which has him assisting in the recovery and rehabilitation of injured marine animals including seals, whales, dolphins, and turtles.

Through his fishing career Mark has guided his friends, clients (and wife) to 17 IGFA world records and eight Maryland state shark records. More importantly, through tagging, sampling, data collection, and assisting in special projects, Mark has been able to assist marine scientists gain a better understanding of the habits, biology, and conservation needs of sharks.

Beside his sport fishing charters, Mark runs "Educational Shark Encounters," where he takes the public offshore to see, tag, and learn about sharks firsthand from the deck of his boat *Fish Finder*.

More information about Captain Mark Sampson and his charter services can be found at www.BigSharks.com

Captain Mark Sampson

Geared Up is dedicated to bringing saltwater anglers the how-to/where-to information that to date has been impossible to get without putting in years and years of fishing and networking among professional anglers. The books published by Geared Up are full of tricks, tips and tactics that professional captains and serious anglers usually keep to themselves. Our goal is bringing you the real word, no BS saltwater fishing information you just can't get anywhere else. If you want to read entertaining fishing stories, get Hemmingway. If you want hard-core how-to/where-to fishing information, get Geared Up's books at our website (www.getgup.com or www.gearedduppublications.com) and in fine tackle shops and book stores. And, we offer the following guarantee: If these books don't help you catch more fish, we'll eat our bait!

GEARED UP PUBLICATIONS, LLC
EDGEWATER, MD
WWW.GEAREDUPPUBLICATIONS.COM

Rudow's Guide To
FISHING THE MID ATLANTIC
38 Charts with More Than 300 Hot Spots!
COASTAL BAYS & OCEAN
By Lenny Rudow

FLOUNDER
Fishing Tactics and Techniques

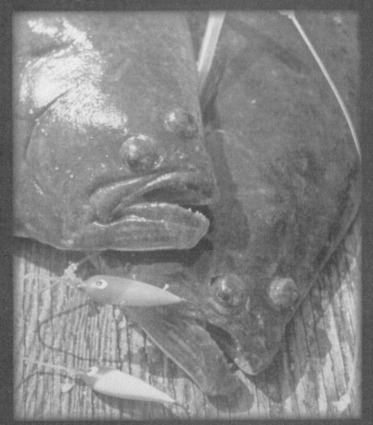

Keith Kaufman

*Former Managing Editor of The Fisherman Magazine and Field
Editor for Chesapeake Angler and The Fisherman Magazines*

RUDOW'S GUIDE TO

ROCK FISH

BY LENNY RUDOW

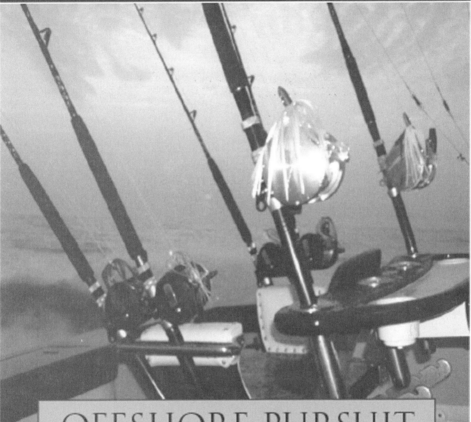

OFFSHORE PURSUIT

BILLFISH · TUNA · WAHOO · MAHI-MAHI

OFFSHORE RIGGING AND TACTICS BY A PROFESSIONAL
WITH 40 YEARS OF EXPERIENCE

BY JOHN UNKART